PETERSEN'S

HUNTING
Guide to
BIG
GAME

PETERSEN'S

HUNTING
Guide to
BIG
GAME

A COMPREHENSIVE GUIDE TO HUNTING ELK, DEER, BEARS, MOOSE, AND MUCH MORE

INTRODUCTION BY MIKE SCHOBY

Skyhorse Publishing

Skyhorse Publishing books may be purchased in bulk at special discounts for sales promotion, corporate gifts, fund-raising, or educational purposes. Special editions can also be created to specifications. For details, contact the Special Sales Department, Skyhorse Publishing, 307 West 36th Street, 11th Floor, New York, NY 10018 or info@skyhorsepublishing.com.

Skyhorse® and Skyhorse Publishing® are registered trademarks of Skyhorse Publishing, Inc.®, a Delaware corporation.

Visit our website at www.skyhorsepublishing.com.

10 9 8 7 6 5 4 3 2 1

Library of Congress Cataloging-in-Publication Data is available on file.

Cover design by Tom Lau
Cover photo credit: Dale C. Spartas

Print ISBN: 978-1-5107-1311-6
Ebook ISBN: 978-1-5107-1317-8

Printed in China

TABLE OF CONTENTS

INTRODUCTION

When I was in my early teens, *Petersen's Hunting* was my bible. I read each month's issue from cover to cover probably within a day of receiving it. More so than all the other sporting magazines of the day, PH ignited my fire for big game hunting and made me dream of hallowed hunting grounds near and far. Not only did it provide a monthly source of entertainment, I learned a lot as well from knowledgeable guys like John Wooters, Gary Sitton, Bob Milek and, of course ,the dean of them all, editor Craig Boddington.

I really didn't know what an editor of Petersen's Hunting did, or how one would get such a job, but I knew I wanted to live his life and I wondered how someone could ever get paid to hunt, which is what his life looked like then (and come to think of it now, actually). But those were just prepubescent dreams, and never did I think I would get the chance to hunt around the world or see Africa or run a hunting magazine.

Time passed and I did what tens of thousands of passionate *Petersen's Hunting* readers do everyday. I hunted—hard. I probably spent five days out of seven before work, after work, and of course every weekend somewhere afield—more often than not sleeping in the back of my old pickup.

My college of choice, Washington State University, was selected not for the renowned Edward R. Murrow School of Communication, but because of the pheasants and mule deer and coyotes visible from campus. I majored in hunting and minored in fishing—and barely escaped after four years with a diploma.

After a couple of decades of spending nearly every waking moment either hunting, thinking about hunting, reading about hunting, or writing about it, I ended up taking the place at the helm of the very magazine I grew up idolizing. That was eight years ago. Both the magazine and I are turning forty-three this year. Not old by any stretch, but old enough for me to ponder what is in store for the next generation.

Yes, I know I sound a lot like Dana Carvey's *Saturday Night Live* character, The Grumpy Old Man, but when I grew up reading *Petersen's Hunting*, there was no Internet, no Facebook, no YouTube or Instagram. If you wanted to learn something about a subject, say hunting, there were books and magazines and hard-won personal experience—that was it. So in today's digital age where everything you ever want to know (and some things you didn't) is just a click away, how relevant is a book or a magazine? I'd say, very.

In fact, I think printed hunting information is more relevant and important than ever before, for one reason: quality of information. While the Internet has brought us quantity what it lacks is quality. *The Rime of the Ancient Mariner*, written over two hundred years ago, reflects today's landscape of information pretty accurately: "Water water everywhere, nor any drop to drink." There is hunting information everywhere, but most of it is of dubious quality, legitimacy, and value. The Internet is rife with writers pontificating over dangerous game guns who have never stepped foot on the African continent. There are plenty of YouTube videos showing how to gut a deer, but the problem is many times it is the video producer's first time doing it.

That is the price of democracy of information where everyone gets to post their opinions/thoughts/knowledge, but much of it isn't worth the free price it came with. Because of that, hunters still yearn for quality information from experienced outdoorsmen. For forty-two years, *Petersen's Hunting* magazine has been educating, informing, and entertaining hunters by providing reliable, quality content. That has not changed in the digital age.

Today, an entirely new crop of hunters are entering the field, many for the first time. Their motivations vary. Some are driven by a desire to leave a suburban or increasingly urban lifestyle to reconnect with ancient primal instincts.

Some posses a desire to connect with their food and the life of the animal that provided it. Some come from the locavore movement and purely want healthy, chemical-free meat. Women are also entering the hunting fields, many for the first time, without growing up in the traditional father/son hunting mentor program. What all these new hunters need is solid, reliable information they can trust, not Internet advice they are too inexperienced to discern as bad.

In this book, our goal was to provide the reader a primer to the main big game species of North America: mule deer, caribou, cougar, predators, black bears, blacktail deer, pronghorn, wild hogs, elk, moose, gators, wolves, big horn sheep, and some whitetail. The next book in the *Petersen's Hunting series* will be devoted solely to whitetail.

We have an amazing line up of stories from past *Petersen's Hunting* magazines by several fine writers. As an aside, there are two writers included in this book who have passed away; Greg Rodriguez and J. Guthrie. Both were personal friends of mine, fantastic writers and who went way too early in life. Rereading their stories reminded me what a talent they both were and that they will sorely be missed.

So without further ado, please enjoy *Petersen's Hunting Guide to Big Game*. Hopefully it will entertain and inform in the grand tradition of *Petersen's Hunting* magazine.

Best,
Mike Schoby
Editor, *Petersen's Hunting* Magazine

MULE DEER FOR MOST OF US

While the West is changing, mule deer are still available.

JOHN BARSNESS

Just a few decades ago mule deer were the commoner's big-game adventure. Even nonresidents could buy tags over the counter and expect to take good bucks. Heck, some states allowed two bucks per season. Today few states sell over-the-counter nonresident tags, and it may take several years to draw a general tag, much less a permit for a super-area such as the Arizona Strip.

The bucks living long enough to grow huge antlers either live in places such as the Strip, where extremely limited tags assure that a few bucks will live past adolescence or on private ranches. Today the ranches offering a chance of a 30-inch mule deer charge prices that may exceed the price of a Dall's sheep hunt. I've hunted such ranches, from Alberta to Sonora, just often enough to know they are a very different world than hunting public-land mule deer in the 21st century.

Luckily, there's still plenty of good mule deer hunting for average hunters. I live in Montana and hunt mule deer on public land almost every year, and I often hunt other states as well. To find mature bucks, however, requires more than just hunting a

likely-looking area. If an area looks good to you, it will also look good to dozens of other hunters.

One basic rule is that more deer live on the plains than in the mountains, but a higher percentage of mountain bucks live long enough

Photo Credit: Dusan Smetana

to grow bigger antlers. There are more places to hide on a rugged mountain than on the relatively flat plains, and uphill hiking keeps most hunters off at least some mountains.

Also, there's a deer gap on many mountains. The foothills and lower ridges often have good populations of deer, but they'll mostly be does, fawns and young bucks. They live there because more deer food grows at lower elevations. Above these low-elevation deer will often be an almost deer-free zone. Then, above that, deer start to show up again. There won't be many, but the bucks will average older and bigger, and they'll live up there until snow and the rut bring them down to the lowland doe herds. The deer gap discourages many hunters who start climbing a mountain and eventually quit seeing deer sign, turning back before they reach the high buck country.

One periodic problem with mountain hunting is winter kill. Mature bucks and fawns are most susceptible to deep snow and cold because the fawns are so small and the bucks are worn down by the fall rut. Deer-killing winters occur more frequently in the mountains than on the plains. I used to guide in a small mountain range in central Montana. One year, a severe winter followed a summer drought. The next fall, finding any sort of mature buck became difficult, and it wasn't hard to see the reason why: There we so many skulls of winter-killed older bucks scattered around the landscape that eventually I wouldn't even hike across a small draw to pick up another.

Hard winters not only kill a lot of big bucks, they kill off the fawn crop that starts to produce mature bucks three to four years later. As a result, before committing yourself to any area, research the recent winters. Game departments can help here, but make sure you talk to an actual biologist, not just an information officer or other indoor help.

Some parts of the plains are also rugged enough to keep out average hunters, particularly the breaks along major rivers and reservoirs. This is typical Bureau of Land Management semi-desert that's too steep and rugged for most hunters— the reason bigger bucks live there. Many of these areas can be accessed by boat, a technique relatively few Western hunters use. The boat doesn't even have to be motorized. Friends and I have been canoe hunting along rivers for many years, reaching parcels of public land far from any road.

However, good bucks can still be found even in places not so difficult to access. If the country's big enough, mature bucks will find places to hide from average hunters. All you have to do is pattern those other hunters and hunt where they don't.

A perfect example is a Colorado hunt an Eastern friend and I made a few years ago. His name is also John, but since he's at least six inches taller than me we'll call him Big John. We hunted a mountain ridge several miles long in the dry northwestern corner of the state. Unlike the higher, snowier mountains farther south in Colorado, this ridge had little timber. Most of the trees were aspens, in a series of long draws that cut the face of the ridge.

On opening morning, Big John was eager to hike the entire ridge. Instead, I told him to get in his rental SUV and follow me. I drove my pickup up a gravel road that headed up the valley alongside the ridge. Sometimes the road followed the little creek in the valley bottom, and other times it rose higher along the hillsides. We parked on a high bend in the road and started glassing.

Partly we glassed for deer, but mostly we glassed for other hunters. They showed up before dawn, most of them driving pickups along the road running the length of the ridge top and occasionally driving ATVs down the side ridges between the aspen canyons. We saw very few hunters actually getting out and walking.

By evening we'd pinpointed where the other hunters didn't go: the lower ends of the big aspen draws. That evening we parked Big John's rental vehicle on the valley road, at the bottom of one of the big draws, then drove my pickup up the big ridge-top road, parking at the head of the same draw.

We got out and slowly hunted downhill. Instead of trying to move deer out of the aspens, we tried to

This is public land big enough to hold a big mule deer.
Photo Credit: John Barsness

make them move away from one of us. I'd hunt downhill on one side of the draw for 200 yards while John stood still on the other side, then when I stopped, he still-hunted until he was 200 yards downhill from me. Toward the bottom of the aspens, a decent 4x4 came out of a thicker patch of trees and stood 100 yards from me—looking toward where John was moving. I passed up the buck, hoping for better things to come.

Soon the aspens petered out, and we were left with a quarter-mile of sagebrush draw before reaching the road where we'd parked Big John's vehicle. As I eased into the tall sage, a buck jumped 30 yards in front of me and in two bounces went around the end of the ridge. I ran to the top of the ridge and just caught a glimpse of him trotting over the horizon 300 yards away, headed for the next aspen draw to the east, his antlers high and heavy against the pale sky.

There wasn't enough time to go after him that evening, but as we hiked down to the road I smiled to myself. The buck bedded where very few hunters would ever go, way down the canyon from the ridge-top road and a few hundred yards above the canyon-bottom road, where he'd be hidden both by the curve of the land and the waist-high sage. He'd probably listened to several dozen vehicles pass below him that day—including my truck.

The next morning we made essentially the same hunt, but in the next draw over, where the buck had run. A few inches of snow had fallen during the night, then the sky cleared. This draw didn't have many aspens, so we hunted farther back from the edge, carefully glassing before taking another few steps and glassing again. Soon I saw a few deer in a thin stand of aspens across the draw, looking almost black against the new snow. In my binocular one turned out to be a buck looking a lot like the one we jumped the evening before, bedded among several feeding does and fawns. It was the third day of November, and he'd found some female company. The stalk turned into a 200-yard, hands-and-knees crawl through the snow, ending in a patch of low sagebrush on a hill across the draw from the little herd of deer. At the snow-dulled report of my .30-06 the buck jumped to his feet, then wobbled and collapsed back into his bed. He turned out to

be a heavy-antlered old 3x3, and it took the rest of the morning to drag him a mile down the draw to the lower road. Luckily, fresh snow makes dragging even a big buck relatively easy.

We found Big John's buck that evening, as he came out of a cliff-steep draw to investigate some doe herds. This was a classic Colorado buck, a wide-antlered 4x4. However, by the time we'd stalked into position above him, he'd lost interest in the does and

Despite what we hear about 30-inch mule deer, there's nothing wrong with a basic mule deer buck on public land—a typical 4x4 with a spread of about 24 inches.
Photo Credit: John Barsness

disappeared into his private draw for the night.

The next morning we split up, me to glass from a distance while Big John hunted the same doe herds the buck had sniffed the afternoon before. I had barely settled into a good rimrock seat, binocular in hand, when I heard a shot from Big John's direction. The buck had wandered out among the

first doe herd he had glassed, 150 yards below him. It doesn't always work out that way, of course, but it did on that hunt.

On another occasion in Montana, a hunter actually pushed a buck to me. I was in the right place at the right time, lying down behind a rimrock sagebrush overlooking a huge Missouri Breaks canyon, the sun just rising behind my shoulder, when I spotted a good 4x4 bedded halfway down the opposite side of the canyon. I was figuring out how to make the stalk when a pickup parked on the top of the opposite side of the canyon. I heard the door slam, faintly, even from a mile away. The hunter started walking right down the nearest ridge top, in full view, and my buck stood up and disappeared downhill. In about a half-hour, however, he came sneaking along the game trail 150 yards below me. Bang! Thank you, unknown hunter.

There are ways to avoid hunters even in accessible country. Montana, for instance, has a five-week rifle season running from late October to the weekend after Thanksgiving. At least 90 percent of hunting pressure takes place during a single week: the first three days of the season and the last four days, starting on Thanksgiving. During the rest of the season you can often hunt midweek and not see another hunter, especially in the areas more than 100 miles from what pass for cities in this part of the world.

Jay Rightnour and I did exactly that one fall, putting up a tent camp in the big badlands of eastern Montana during the second week of November. We never saw another hunter, and Jay took his first good mule deer buck on

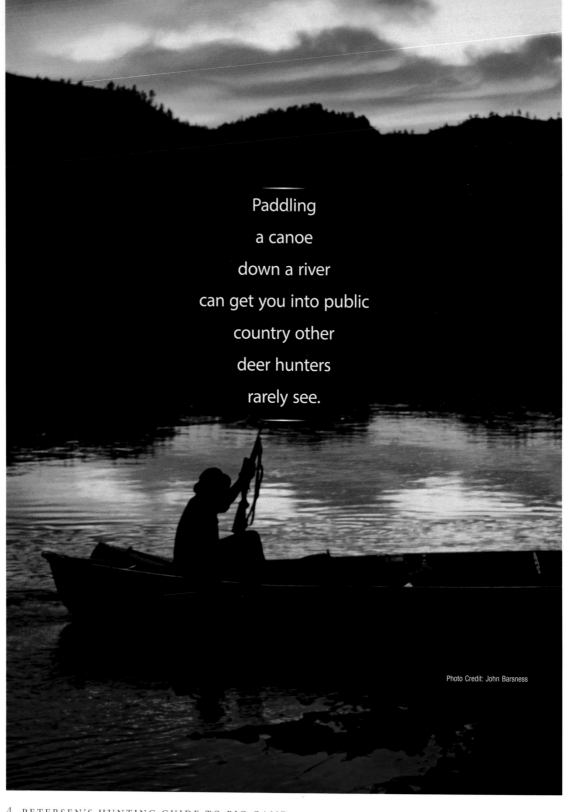

Paddling

a canoe

down a river

can get you into public

country other

deer hunters

rarely see.

Photo Credit: John Barsness

TOP LEFT

Jay Rightnour took this nice buck on BLM land during the middle of the Montana rifle season, when hunting pressure drops off.

TOP RIGHT

The author's wife found this nice 3x3 on public land in Montana. Older bucks such as this one often grow fewer tines on their antlers.

BOTTOM LEFT

The author took this big 6x6 on a public-land outfitted hunt in Montana, right at timberline.

BOTTOM RIGHT

The author killed his first big mountain mule deer over 30 years ago by hiking uphill through the "deer gap." The buck's antlers weren't exceptional, but he weighed nearly 250 pounds field-dressed.

Photo Credit: John Barsness

Photo Credit: John Barsness

the fourth day of the hunt, after a mile-long stalk. We eventually ended up a little more than 100 yards from the bedded buck, with nobody around except a few coyotes that sounded off as we packed out the buck by the last light of sunset.

Another option is to pay for a drop-camp in the mountains, or even a guided hunt. On public land even a guided hunt will cost only a quarter as much as one on an exclusive private ranch. The big trick, however, is to find an outfitter who really understands mule deer. Most outfitters who guide on Forest Service land are elk-oriented, because that's what most customers want, and good elk country usually isn't the best mule deer country.

The second thing is to have faith. Mule deer aren't abundant in the high country, but that's where the really big ones live. I killed my biggest buck ever, both in body and antler, while on a horseback hunt with an outfitter I used to occasionally help during his summer pack trips. Jackson is gone now, the victim of one of his own horses and a steep trail, so I am very glad we had that week together. We only saw four deer the entire week, but they were all mature bucks, up around timberline, far from the elk timber down below.

How big a buck can you expect to find? Once in awhile you might find a huge one, especially in the mountains, but on most public land I feel very happy with what one of my friends calls "the basic muley buck," a typical 4x4 with antlers around 24 inches wide. Any public buck with some antler mass, or a spread over 25 inches, is a real trophy. In fact, I have been quite proud to take some big 3x3 bucks. That old Colorado buck had antler bases I could barely circle with my hand, and one Wyoming 3x3 had a 28-inch spread. Often bucks grow fewer tines as they age, and any truly mature buck is a trophy no matter what his antlers score. ⓑ

John Barsness writes about the outdoors from his home in Montana, partly with his wife Eileen Clarke (also an avid hunter who's published ten game cookbooks) on their website, www.riflesandrecipes.com.

MOUNTAIN
CARIBOU
OF THE CASSIARS

Inhospitable country, horses and
a few mistakes combine for an
adventure of a lifetime.

WORDS & IMAGES by
MIKE SCHOBY

Like a flash from a camera, the

spark illuminated the inky darkness, etching itself onto my retina. Before my brain could register the source of the spark, I heard the noise. It sounded like rocks being ground together in a miniature crusher, but what it sounded like and what my fatigued gray matter knew it was were two different things. Unmistakably, the spark and the grinding noise were a horse's shoes skidding and sliding across granite. A fresh bloom of sparks flashed in front of me, and I heard my guide, Kyle Serle, trying to sooth his whinnying horse.

As sparks danced like imaginary stars in the pitch-black darkness, I reached for the button on my headlamp. The blinding-white halogen beam contracted my pupils and wrecked my night vision, but illuminated the trail in front of me as well as to my left where the jagged granite rock hemmed in close to the horse's whither. To my right there was nothing, just more inky blackness. My horse stepped on a loose rock, and I watched as the stone rolled off the side of the narrow ledge disappearing into the black abyss, only to echo its crash to the ground hundreds of feet below. The horse shook his head in disapproval—he didn't like the situation any more than I did.

Deciding to fall off the cliff on my own two feet instead of on the back of my horse, I quickly dismounted, grabbed the halter rope and led the horse up the ledge. It was touch and go for a hundred yards, and I spent more time on all fours than I did walking upright, but we eventually made it. Upon reaching the top, I noticed Kyle was also dismounted and had a map spread out across his saddle—never a good sign. When he said, "I think we go up this canyon," I had an inclination we might be in trouble. When the wind suddenly flapped the map like a flag in the breeze and sleet stung my face, I knew we were.

I have a bush plane pilot buddy who once told me that plane crashes don't usually happen because of a single thing going wrong. "Problems

each other that led to our current predicament.

The day started out like any of the previous nine others. We woke up in

brush to the lichen-covered rocks on top of the mountains. We quickly tied them, grabbed spotting scopes out of our saddlebags and headed to the promontory that had become our temporary home. Kyle and I took our accustomed spots. By now our butts and backs knew exactly where the most comfortable spots were and which roots and rocks to avoid. After a couple of hours of glassing, seeing the same family groups of animals we had been seeing day in and day out, Kyle said, "Well, we can always head over the pass and see what's on the other side."

"How far is it?" I asked.

"Lets try it. What's the worst that can happen?" I said with a grin. In retrospect, those are words I wished I hadn't uttered.

never come alone, they come in unassuming, minor packs, and it is the accumulation of these problems that builds up to serious problems, which inevitably lead to a crash." The same could be said for our situation. It was several small bad choices piled upon

our tents, caught horses—which, even though hobbled, managed to travel miles in the dark—ate a quick breakfast and headed to the high country to glass for mountain caribou. We had been glassing the same mountain range for the entire week, and while we had spotted a dozen or so animals, there was nothing but cows and calves—the bulls were still farther upcountry.

Our horses were well lathered when they fought through the buck

"It's a long ride, probably several miles, but there is another huge valley over there that might have some caribou." Not having anything else to do, I agreed. The ride over the pass was absolutely stunning. High above timberline, it was a massive boulder field

interspersed with crystal-clear ponds rimmed by the peaks of the mountains. On top of the pass, there was some weather-worn scraps of lumber and unidentifiable rusty iron, left by a long-forgotten prospector. It was an eerie, windswept, lonely place, but the surroundings made you respect the sheer iron will of those early explorers.

By midafternoon we came through the pass, and before us lay a huge valley. Immediately, we spotted a band of caribou—more cows and calves, but a good start. We quickly set up spotting scopes and started looking at virgin country. Our initial luck proved not to hold. There were no other caribou. I was packing up my spotting scope, preparing to move to

another vantage point when Kyle said, "I got a decent bull . . . I think."

I walked over and looked through his scope. The bull was on top of the farthest mountain we could see. Even at 45 power the bull appeared like a speck on the glass, and to be honest, until he turned his head and revealed just the slightest glimmer of reflection, it was hard to tell he was a bull at all.

"How far away do you think he is?" I asked.

"Four maybe five miles."

"You want to go after him?"

"Do you?"

"Well, we haven't seen anything else, and I only have a couple more days to hunt. Do you think we can make it in time?"

"It will be close."

"Let's try it. What's the worst that can happen?" I said with a grin. In retrospect, those are words I wish I hadn't uttered.

We rode through bog, rivers and buck brush higher than a man's head. We swam the horses

Filmed for an episode of Petersen's Hunting Adventures TV, this British Columbia hunt in the Cassiar Mountains turned into a epic wilderness adventure. Discomforts aside, all is well that ends well, and here the author poses with his first mountain caribou.

through a beaver pond. Even with my legs lifted out of the stirrups, my boots got soaked. In the thick timber of the other side, limbs tore at my jacket and ripped holes in one pant leg. On the other side of the valley we rode up ridges so steep we kicked our feet loose from the stirrups, held onto our horse's mane and let our legs swing out past its flanks. Two hours later, we were nearly there.

We stopped the horses just shy of the rim leading into the bowl where we had spotted the bull. Well above tree line with no place to secure the horses, we did the next-best thing and tied them lead to horn before we slowly stalked to the edge. Peering in, the hunting gods were smiling on us, as there was our bull, still feeding, not 300 yards below. He was a good bull, not a great bull, but one to be proud of.

I was using a Marlin Guide Gun in .45-70 topped with a Leupold Shotgun/Muzzleloader scope. Earlier that summer at the range, I worked with a Federal load that not only shot sub-MOA groups—which I found amazing out of the stubby gun—but

meshed perfectly with the ballistic lines of the scope. I tested it out to 300 yards and could consistently hold three-inch groups dead on using the lines. However, that was at the range, not on live game, so I said, "Let's sneak a little closer to get a better shot."

We crouched and crawled through the rocks and low shrubs until we were within a couple hundred yards of the still-feeding bull. Easing over a rock, I set down my daypack and rested the rifle on it. The bull was broadside and unaware of our presence. I peered at

him through the scope and slowly cocked the hammer. I was waiting for my labored breathing to subside and still several seconds away from taking the shot when Kyle whispered, "Hold up. There is a bigger bull over the next ridge."

I lowered the hammer, set down the rifle and grab-bed my binoculars. About 800 yards away another bull fed between two ridges. He was a better bull —how much bigger I wasn't sure, but he was bigger.

"You want to go after him?" Kyle asked.

"Yeah, but it is going to be tough," I replied.

We only had about an hour of shooting light left, and in order to get to this new bull we would have to back off, skirt all the way around the mountain and come up the other side if we wanted to avoid spooking the first bull, which might spook the second.

We decided the risk was worth the reward. After many days of not seeing a shooter bull, lowering the hammer, sliding off the rock perch and sneaking back down the mountain was one of the toughest things I have ever done. My mind kept rolling around the old adage "a bird in the hand is better than a bird in the bush."

It took us all of 45 minutes to get around the side of the mountain and up the small ridge. The top of the ridge turned into a mini-plateau. We got down on hands and knees and crawled across the tabletop-flat surface. With every inch we gained, another few yards of the valley floor below became visible. When nearly all of the valley was exposed and there was no bull in sight, my heart dropped. We should have shot that first bull, I silently cursed myself.

"Right in front of us," Kyle whispered.

I snuck up a few more inches, and sure enough, the bull's antlers came into view. He must have heard us crawling over the rocks, as he was alert and drilling through us with his eyes. I quickly poked the muzzle of the rifle over the ledge and thumbed back the hammer. Realizing something was amiss, the bull spun around, took a few steps, then

Lost in the wilderness with a storm moving in, the hunting party found a patch of timber, made a fire and waited until dawn.

stopped to look back a final time. Now or never, I centered the crosshairs and squeezed the trigger. Hit hard, the bull hunkered up, then started walking away. I worked the lever and centered on his rear hip joint so the bullet would angle through the chest. The second bullet performed as expected, and the bull dropped in its tracks.

As with any big-game hunt anywhere in the world, as soon as the animal is down, the hunt is over and the work begins. With 30 minutes until dark, we snapped a few photos and got busy skinning, quartering and caping the bull. We finished with a few minutes of light

left. I was for staying close to the kill scene, building a small campfire and waiting out the night, but Kyle said, "Look, the horses can find their way back to camp in the dark, and they can see fine at night." This fact is still debated, but it ultimately proved to be our downfall.

Two hours later we were back on top of the mountain, searching for the lost pass that would take us back to camp and wondering how we got ourself into this situation. As I said before, it is the small problems that tend to be your downfall. With sleet now pounding down, Kyle said, "I think this canyon is the way across the pass." Leading our horses, head

lamps now constantly on, we started to climb. As we gained elevation with every step, the wind increased, the temperature dropped and the sleet turned to a rain/snow mixture. An hour into the climb, we leveled out into a large basin well above treeline, and while it looked similar to the pass we crossed earlier in the day, we both knew it wasn't. Not exactly sure which way camp was and with a gale blowing at this higher elevation, we decided to call a halt to the march. We dropped down a little in elevation and found a lone outcropping of stunted evergreen trees. They grew in a thick clump no more than 20 yards in diameter. They didn't provide much cover from the impending storm, but they provided enough. We tied up the horses and headed into the thick of the Christmas-tree-size evergreens. Clearing a small area of low-hanging limbs, we hunkered down and set to work starting a fire with

soaking-wet tree limbs. With the help of some fire starters and a little luck, we succeeded. We strung a reflective space blanket between two trees to serve as a windbreak and settled down to spend the night, alternating between fitful sleep and waking up freezing to stoke the fire.

Dawn finally broke, but it seemed to take an eternity. The surrounding mountains were glistening white, covered in a fresh dumping of snow. In the early-morning light it was easy to see where we had gone wrong. We were one pass off from the correct one, which in this part of the world made all the difference. Tightening the cinch straps on the horses, we saddled up and started our several-mile ride back to camp. Other than the nearly hypothermic conditions, the ride was uneventful and we arrived by midmorning. Cold and soaked through, we wolfed down some hot soup and collapsed into the relative warmth of our clammy sleeping bags.

The next couple of days were spent packing out to a pick-up point on a lake where the DeHavilland Beaver would come to take us back to civilization. At the lake, we found an old hunting cabin. The contents were ravaged by a mink or weasel, while the door had gone a few rounds with a determined bear, but there was dry wood under the eves and a working tin stove inside. To us it looked like the Ritz, and for the first time in two weeks we slept like hibernating bears while the wind howled outside.

Part of me wanted to get home. I was anxious for my first shower in two weeks, a meal at a table and the comfort of a good bed, but part of me wanted to stay up in the wilds of the Cassiars, shivering on a horse, heating a piece of meat over a smoldering fire and seeing what lay over the next ridge. As they say, all's well that ends well, and our little experience left none of us worse for wear, but if another problem or two would have cropped up, a serious situation could have turned critical. That's the allure of the wilderness.

It's not predictable, it's seldom comfortable, but it's always exciting.— *bcsafaris.com* Ⓗ

FOUR FEET ON 7

Sometimes Rocky Mountain cat hunting is about paying your dues.

I MET UP with Alice Pulochova, president of CZ-USA, in Grand Junction, Colorado. It was mid-February, and the snow fell in a quiet blanket as we drove toward the quaint mountain town of Rifle. Our plan was simple and straightforward. Alice and I were to spend a week chasing mountain lions with outfitter Andy Julius. You could say that Alice kind of has a thing for big cats. She had taken a beautiful lioness in South Africa back in 2005 and a great leopard in Namibia the previous year, but so far, after three attempts at mountain lions, she had gone home empty-handed. Hence, we booked a trip with Andy. I had heard about Andy through a friend who knows good outfitters from bad. This friend had hunted with Andy a couple of times and raved about him, which was good enough for me.

When we arrived and met Andy, I easily saw why my friend was so impressed with him. You could tell immediately that Andy was passionate about hunting lions. Covered in dog hair from head to toe and looking slightly disheveled as well as sleep deprived, he had been hard after cats for the better part of the past 48 hours. "You guys got here at the perfect time. We had a few inches of snow two nights ago, and it has been clear ever since. The cats have been out making tracks. I've been up the last two days straight, taking naps in the truck when I get too tired, looking for tracks, and I have a couple of big males isolated in two different canyons."

Excited by the fantastic news, we hurriedly unpacked our gear and got ready for the following day's hunt. After our clothes were unpacked and sorted out, we headed out to the back of the lodge to the makeshift gun range. Opening up a small case, Alice withdrew a dead-sexy stainless steel, full-size 1911. On the side was written "Dan Wesson." Being somewhat of an amateur competitive pistol shooter in my youth, I was familiar with the Dan Wesson brand, made famous by its revolvers with interchangeable barrels, but this was the first time I got to fondle one of the company's new autos.

John Browning's famous 1911 pistol is often thought of in one of two ways, either as a competitive pistol for one of the many shooting disciplines or as a defensive arm for military, police and civilians alike. Rarely is it thought of as a hunting gun.

HE LEVEL

WORDS & IMAGES by
MIKE SCHOBY

IN THE truest sense of the word, it probably isn't a hunting handgun, but over the years I have found plenty of hunting opportunities where the venerable 1911 is just the right ticket. Off and on for the past 20 years, I have carried a 1911 in the field and found numerous occasions to employ it, from coyotes and jackrabbits to ground hogs and even one unlucky black bear. The 1911 shines afield because it is easy to carry and easier to shoot. Loaded with +P cartridges with expanding bullets, it can serve well as a medium-size game gun—if the ranges are kept close. In my experience, it has always worked to a T, and the real-world ballistic results overshadowed what the paper foot-pounds would suggest it is capable of. As Elmer Keith knew, there is something to be said for a slow-moving, big, heavy bullet, energy tables be damned.

"When we bought Dan Wesson and decided to start building 1911s in 2005, we didn't want to create just another 'me, too' model. We wanted to build the best 1911 possible. I think we succeeded," Alice informed me. Holding the gun, I had to agree.

The slide-to-frame fit was precise and tight, as was the fit of barrel to bushing in front. The overall fit was Swiss-watch perfect and indicated a quality build-up, one that involved lots of hand-fitting. As I turned over the gun, admiring it from every angle, cool features just kept popping out at me. In fact, to a guy like me who enjoys occasionally building a 1911, it was almost disheartening—there was

really nothing left to customize. It appeared that every 1911 problem had been polished out of the Dan Wesson line. Features such as Heinie sights, custom stocks, precisely fit Ed Brown beavertail, flared ejection port, polished barrel throat, extended safety, match barrel and checkered mainspring housing and frontstrap rounded out the package. If the gun shot as well as it looked, I knew my checkbook was going to feel the bite.

When I asked her if I could try it, Alice handed me a loaded magazine. I inserted the mag in the beveled well and cycled the slide. The round seated home with a precise snick. It is one thing to make a gun tight; it's a

The overall fit was SWISS-WATCH PERFECT and indicated a quality build-up.

completely separate thing to make a gun tight and function well. This gun achieved both. The Heinie sights presented a clean image against the target as I squeezed off the first round. Dead on. A few more rounds just enlarged the hole. Shooting a super-accurate .45 is a lot like shooting the red-star-target game at the fair with a bb machine gun: The hole just gets larger as you see chunks of target disappear. Very pleased with the

results, I handed the Dan Wesson back to Alice with a smile. She checked the gun with a few rounds of her own, with equally satisfying results, and reholstered it.

On this hunt I carried a TenPoint crossbow. I had taken this crossbow on several hunts, from Texas for deer and hogs to Florida for gators and even new Zealand for red deer. It had delivered on all three hunts, and I was anxious to see how it would perform on North America's largest feline. I took a few shots with the TenPoint and confirmed that the Leupold scope was still on after a thousand miles of air travel and a few thousand feet of elevation change.

I grew up around mountain lions in my home state of Washington and held a tag nearly every year I hunted. However, I had never hunted with dogs, so this was a first for me and the plan was for me to get first crack at a cat. Following Andy to the top of a mountain on snow-packed roads, we came upon his partner, Trent Snyder, waiting in a truck, hot coffee in hand. "The track is right over here," he said as we pulled up. As we walked through the knee-deep snow, the track of a large male mountain lion could easily be seen. "It's a day old, but the dogs shouldn't have a problem following him," he continued. With that, he got two dogs out of the box in the bed of the truck, snapped on

Dogs are as much a part of the sport of lion hunting as the cat itself—everything else is secondary. Listening to the hounds hit a fresh track and then bark at a treed animal is a vocal hunting experience second possibly only to a bugling elk.

their leads and took them over to the track. The dogs buried their noses in the first track, went to the second and did it again. By the third track, the lead dog let out a long, drawn-out bawl, and he had the track locked in his mind. Unsnapping the leads, Trent let the dogs run. "Now comes the waiting. It could take anywhere from an hour to a day. It all depends upon how far the cat has traveled since yesterday." We sat back, opened a Thermos of coffee and listened to the dogs work the trail up the valley.

After an hour or so, the dogs were no longer in hearing range, so Alice, Trent and I headed out on foot to see if we could hear them. Andy and his son mounted a snow machine and ATV, respectively, to cut some of the roads surrounding the valley to see if the dogs had followed the cat out of the area.

We had walked for possibly an hour in deep snow and worked our way up to the head of the valley without any sign of the dogs when Trent's radio crackled. Though his voice was garbled, you could hear Andy say, "They jumped the cat . . .

Hot on . . . trail . . . Heading over to the next drainage. Come down . . . mountain . . . Pick you up at the bottom . . . snow machine." The dogs could be heard baying frantically over the airwaves.

Smiling, we started off on the long hike to the bottom. The snow was deep and the hike was long, but at least it was downhill. When we reached the bottom, Andy was waiting for us, and we piled onto the snow machine and the trailer he was towing. It was a rough ride back to the top of the mountain and into the next valley, but it was much easier than walking. We got to the head of the next valley in a little over an hour. Once there, we stopped to listen. Way down in the next drainage you could hear the dogs barking. They had a cat treed. It was like music, and for the first time I understood what the allure of hounds was all about.

We still had a couple of hours until dark. The sun was out, turning the Colorado mountains into a winter wonderland of sparkling snow and blinding white light mixed with the reds and browns of the exposed cliff faces and the verdant green of the evergreens.

Leaving the snow machine, we started to hike. By the time we got close to where the dogs were baying, the late-winter sun had lost its intensity and started its slide toward the horizon, skirting the surrounding mountaintops with its last rays and painting the hills in a golden glow.

Suddenly, we saw the dogs under a gnarled, old juniper, barking and trying to climb the lone ancient tree. As we got closer, the cat could be seen. It was a large male, as we thought, poised just 20 feet off the ground. Even

though the cat was more than I ever dreamed of and was already paid for in sweat, it just didn't feel right. It was my first hunt behind dogs, my first cat in a tree. "Get ready," Andy said. "In small trees like this, cats will often jump. Dogs can get hurt, and even if they don't, we don't have enough daylight left to tree him again." I looked back at Alice and could see the desire in her face. She wanted this cat. Thinking about the beautiful weather, tons of unpressured property and the other cats in the area, I turned to her and said, "Why don't you shoot this cat? I'll get another chance." As soon as I said it, I knew it was the right thing to do. She had paid dearly for this in time and sweat on her other hunts. This was her fourth trip, she'd earned it, and I was happy just to be there as a witness.

She looked shocked, but didn't argue. She simply nodded her head, got in position and drew her 1911 from the shoulder holster. Until now, I don't think any of the cowboys in the party were too sure how she would handle herself with a handgun, but it was easy to see from her two-handed, rock-steady hold that this wasn't her first rodeo. When the dogs were

tethered away from the tree, Andy gave her the go-ahead.

Her first shot hit a branch and deflected; her second shot hit home. The cat stiffened, froze and toppled out of the tree. A cacophony of dogs and hollering people ensued. One look at Alice's face and you could see she was elated. I was elated for her. On a cat hunt, pulling the trigger is only a small part of the experience, and I felt that just by being there I was richer for it. The hard hiking, the tracking, listening to the dogs—it's there for everyone to share, and I was just glad to be along for the ride.

Besides, I had an entire week left of the hunt, and there were plenty of

That night, the snow kept falling. I got up several times to peer out the window into the inky blackness. Across the ranch yard, against the barn light, I could see the ultra-fine snow still falling like Tony Montana's beloved Bolivian marching powder.

On a cat hunt, PULLING THE TRIGGER is only a small part of the experience.

By the last day, four feet had accumulated.

Our days were spent drinking coffee, eating too much and watching it snow. Occasionally, we would discuss politics, sex and religion just to break up the monotony. In the mornings we would drive the few open mountain roads looking for tracks, but Andy was right—nothing was moving. It was hopeless. The tracks were covered with new snow in a matter of hours. I closed out the week empty-handed and headed back to Grand Junction. On the radio the news reported it was the heaviest snowfall to hit the area all winter. I

Alice Pulochova's large male mountain lion. She worked hard on other trips for a cat like this, and this one was a fitting reward for her efforts. Big cats just seem to get bigger when you pick them up and load them on the snow machine for the long ride out.

other cats left in the area. As we loaded up the cat on the snow machine, darkness had almost set and clouds had moved in. The first tendrils of snow lazily drifted down, coating everything in a fresh white powder. "A light dusting of fresh tracking snow will make the hunting even better this week," Andy said as we drove off into the darkness.

By morning we had a fresh foot of snow on the ground, and more was still coming. "In weather like this, the cats will be locked down. We pretty much have to wait until it breaks before the cats start moving again,"

Andy commented over coffee. So we sat and waited . . . for the rest of the week. The snow never did quit.

smiled thinking back to Alice's wonderful cat. She had put in her time for it, not on this trip but on others just like I was now experiencing. I rebooked with Andy, and if I get another chance at a big male tom in a stunted juniper, I will take the shot. I now feel that I have put in my time. ⓗ

THE INSIDE PLAYBOOK

FOR VARSITY PREDATOR HUNTERS

MIKE SCHOBY

After the basics are mastered, here are the top things a hunter needs to know to earn a predator-hunting PhD.

IT IS NO SECRET that predators have an uncanny ability not only to survive, but to thrive in today's ever-changing world. By learning to adapt to human encroachment, many predators—especially coyotes—have spread their range across the entire continental United States, including major cities and suburban areas. But adapting is not just about living with humans, it is about adapting to hunting pressure.

As predator hunting has increased in popularity, predators themselves have gotten tougher to kill. They associate the more common calls with flying bullets instead of dying bunnies. Predators now listen for vehicle traffic and become extremely cautious when it is heard. They have learned to circle downwind before committing to a setup. They hunt hard at night and less and less during the day. If you are seeing these trends, there's little doubt that predators in your area have upped their game. If you want to compete in this evolving and extremely challenging sport, you must follow suit.

Incorporate these advanced techniques into your repertoire to take your calling game to the next level and hopefully put more fur on the stretcher this season.

There is a time and place for loud calling. Look for electronic calls with large, cone-style speakers, or even add on additional amplified speakers to an existing system.

When it comes to killing bobcats, patience is the key. Unlike fox and coyotes, which respond rather quickly to a call, bobcats make take upward of an hour and a half to sneak into range.

AMP UP YOUR CALLING

As winter sets in and wind sweeps across much of the land, turn to more power to reach out and touch predators. Electronic callers are a good start to increase your range, but to really be effective, pick a model that is designed for high volume, such as the Fox Pro Prairie Blaster. If you don't want to invest in an entirely new caller, look at plugging additional speakers with built-in amps into your existing unit to crank up the volume. In addition to pure volume, try changing up your technique for windy-day action. Instead of playing the caller for a few minutes, shutting it down and waiting, try letting it blast at full volume. We have done this on windy-day sets, with the call blowing full volume from the moment we first spotted the dog until he was dead up close, with no ill effects.

WHEN NOT TO USE A DECOY

There is no question that under the right circumstances prey decoys can tip the odds in a hunter's favor. They can convince wary coyotes to close the distance and dupe them into range. They can also keep a predator's attention off the hunter if a small shift in movement has to be made to take the shot. Most of the time decoys are good, but occasionally they are not. Sometimes making the effort to set up a decoy may actually expose you to more predators than it will help you bag, spooking the whole setup before the first note is blown. Advanced predator callers understand this and know when to use decoys and when not to. A few general rules: Always set a decoy if cats are sought. Always set a decoy if there are concealed approach alleys. Always set a decoy if you think you may have to move for a shot. Always set a decoy if

experience in the area suggests coyotes will hang up out of range. In all other cases, examine the sets carefully and decide if placing a decoy is worth the risk. If it is not, skip it and you may be more successful.

SONG DOG DOUBLE DOWN

Beginning hunters are more than happy calling in and killing a single coyote, as they should be. But like good pool players, advanced hunters are not thinking so much about killing a single coyote as setting up their next shot. When multiple dogs come into a call, try to take the farthest one first. The closer one will likely stop in range if wounded coyote calls are made immediately after the shot. Even if a single comes in, it is a good practice to immediately switch from a prey-in-distress call to a wounded coyote or pup-in-distress call as soon as the shooting starts. If you are hand-

Carry two guns into every stand: a shotgun loaded with BBs or T shot and a flat-shooting rifle. With both options you have every scenario covered from close in to long range.

calling, keep both calls at the ready. If you are using an electronic call, take a look at the Fox Pro calls with Fox Bang; it detects the shot and immediately switches over to a secondary sound such as a wounded coyote. Keep calling with a wounded coyote call for up to 10 minutes. It's amazing how many times a secondary unseen coyote will cautiously emerge.

WAITING THEM OUT

Most coyote hunters feel that 15 minutes is plenty of time to allow a coyote to reach a stand. If a coyote takes longer than this, your time may be better spent hitting another area, but for cats, be prepared to stick it out much longer. Consider 45 minutes more the norm, with an hour and a half not being unreasonable. Scan the foreground carefully. More often than not, a cat will sneak into range without being noticed. Visual attraction combined with high-pitched sounds are the key for kitties. "I have watched

Photo Credit: windigoimages.com–Mark Kayser

Beat the rush and head out predator hunting early in the year. In some cases you may have to hunt around deer season (and abide by certain restrictions such as blaze orange), but the results are worth it.

Know when and when not to use decoys. In many situations decoys can help—such as this set for bobcats. However, in extremely open country they may expose hunters to spooky coyotes.

cats come in and if they don't see something, they will often turn around and sneak back out," says Mark Zepp of Zepp Game Calls. "But if there is something to catch their eye—and it can be anything from a motorized decoy to a feather to a piece of toilet paper—you will hook them."

STRING OUT STANDS

One of the keys to killing lots of predators is not only having multiple prime calling stands, but having them located in a route that allows for easy access. Look for a series of sets a mile or two apart that feature minimum walking time from the truck to the actual calling spot. Remember, time spent walking into a stand takes away from calling time and gives predators a better chance of spotting you crossing open ground. If you have a string of spots separated by a couple of miles, you can make hay. If you have one good stand, then must drive across the

county to reach a second stand, valuable time is wasted behind the windshield.

A GUN FOR EACH HAND

Try a two-gun approach this season and watch your success rates climb. At certain times a flat-shooting rifle is ideal predator medicine. At others the killing field is measured in feet, not yards, and a shotgun is a better tool for the job. Whichever you choose, invariably you will have the wrong gun at hand. The answer is to carry two to every stand. "I sometimes carry two guns afield," says Fred Eichler of Predator Nation Television. "One is a shotgun, and the other is my Rock River AR-15." Affix a bipod and set up the rifle next to you. Hold a shotgun in your lap. Something along the lines of a 12-gauge pistol-grip autoloader with Federal copper-coated BBs or Dead Coyote T's and an extra-full choke is ideal. If a predator pops up at spitting range, you are covered, and

if it appears at distance, you have time to set down the scattergun and slowly pick up the rifle. Carrying the extra half dozen pounds will be worth it for the extra weight you will end up dragging out each day.

BIGGER IS BETTER

We all love pelts with tiny .17- or .22-caliber holes in them, but sometimes if you really want to kill predators you have to step up the bore diameter. It's a simple fact that bigger calibers such as .243 Winchester, .240 Weatherby and 6mm Remington are better performers at long range than smaller calibers. For most predators, anything from .243 to .260 caliber is ideal. They buck the wind better, carry more energy, offer a flat trajectory and can increase your effective range, adding up to more pelts on the stretcher. The tradeoff? A bigger hole and more stitching if you keep the pelt, but at least you have a predator to skin.

NIGHT MOVES

Calling predators after sunset is not an easy technique to learn, but once it is mastered, it can be extremely productive. This is especially true in areas where predators receive heavy hunting pressure or when the daytime temperatures are mild, keeping animals nocturnal. The key is to use a two-hunter approach, with one hunter calling and scanning with a red-lens spotlight and the shooter set up beside the caller. The shooter should have an intense light such as the SureFire M3LT flashlight affixed directly to the scope with a pressure on/off switch. Since limited areas can be covered with the light, pick setups that have defined approach lanes. On top of a small cut bank overlooking a creek bottom is a good example. Limiting their approach lanes reduces the chance of animals sneaking in the back door and funnels them in within range.

BEAT A DIFFERENT DRUM

In heavily hunted areas, skip the cottontail and jack-in-distress calls. In many cases too many hunters are using the same call and have educated the coyotes. Pat Muffler, Pro Staff for Hunter Specialties, says, "I like strange calls like the yellow hammer woodpecker in distress. Everyone goes to the dying rabbit, but the yellow hammer woodpecker is rarely heard. In a Johnny Stewart electronic caller, I have found that it works for everything from coyotes to foxes to bobcats."

JUMP THE GUN

Most hunters wait until after all other seasons are over before they head out to try their hand at predators. This used to be a good idea. With cold weather increasing predators' activity as well as thickening their coats, winter was the ideal time. Now, however, with more educated predators, hunters should try earlier than ever before. If you want a crack at uneducated song dogs, break out the calls in October and November when everyone is out deer and bird hunting. In most regions you will be met with moderate weather, no hunting pressure and very responsive 'yotes.

NONTRADITIONAL SETS

When it comes to bagging lots of predators, keep an eye out for nontraditional places. This means considering parks where hunting is allowed, suburban areas seldom hunted and even frozen lakes, as Muffler discovered. "I do a lot of hunting on frozen lakes in the north country, and it is amazing how many coyotes will travel the ice. It seems like it is no-man's land. Coyotes are so territorial, but on the ice it is a free-for-all. Add some calling with some bait [where legal] and in some cases a deer decoy half buried in the snow and you will find that hunting the ice can be an incredible experience."

Predators have always been a challenge, some say the biggest challenge, to hunt. They are satisfying when fooled and frustrating when not. With these tips, not only will you be able to fool them more than ever before, you'll be able to add the smart ones to the bag as well. Ⓗ

Photo credit: windigoimages.com–Mitch Kezar

A DIFFERENT Approach FOR Mulies

{ DOES CALLING MULE DEER REALLY WORK? }

WORDS & IMAGES by
GREG RODRIGUEZ

I COULDN'T BELIEVE the line of b.s. outfitter Hunter Ross was spewing as we stumbled our way up and down the rocky slopes of the Davis Mountains on that coal-dark night. His nonsensical ramblings about calling in monster mulies with a simple mouth call were driving me crazy. We were laboring under the burden of uneven terrain and the weight of our packs, which were bursting at the seams thanks to the massive aoudad ram I'd shot at last light, and we'd run out of water hours before. It was still over 90 degrees at 10 p.m., and I was parched, hungry and exhausted from climbing all day in the

The author and his crew did a bit of glassing, but they spent most of their time bouncing from call site to call site in this little Jeep. Their run-and-gun style put them on as many as 15 bucks in a single day—more than the average Sonora hunter sees in an entire week.

searing West Texas heat. I really wasn't in the mood for Hunter's wild stories.

We eventually made it back to Hunter's truck, where we gulped down every water bottle and Gatorade in the cooler, then went on to the house where we sat up and argued all night about calling mule deer. To shut him up, I agreed to hunt with him in Mexico the following season. I promptly forgot all about it until Hunter called me the following November and said, "Hey, I have two weeks available in January. Which one do you want?"

I stammered and stumbled for a minute, but I sort of recalled those fuzzy, whiskey-fueled conversations and Hunter's promise to prove his calling abilities. I booked my flights while we talked and gave Hunter my gun info so he could organize my permits, then I retired to my easy chair

to contemplate the wisdom of hunting with an outfitter who was clearly delusional.

Shortly before my hunt, Hunter called to let me know he'd be late getting to camp because he had some family business to attend to. He said that Troy Calaway, his top guide, was going to

take care of me and my hunting partner. If I hadn't known Hunter for so long, the last-minute change would have made me really nervous, but he has always delivered for me and my clients in the past. I wasn't the least bit surprised to find Troy waiting at the airport with our gun permits in hand. We were zipping north

to the ranch where we hoped to find a monster mulie.

Troy didn't talk about calling deer on the drive, and I didn't mention it. I figured Hunter had been pulling my leg about the deer calling, but he has an excellent track record of producing monster bucks for his clients, so I decided to go with the flow. I figured we'd go out and glass for deer in the morning like most hunters do, and if I got lucky, I'd see a big one before the end of the week.

We'd sighted-in our rifles the night before, so we headed out well before sunrise the first day. The predawn chill had a bite up on the high rack of the Jeep, but we didn't drive too long before we parked just below the crest of a hill to begin our hunt. I broke out my big Zeiss and tried to get a view of the surrounding area, but I couldn't see much. Once the sun rose, I saw why. Rather than glassing huge open areas, Troy had set us up against a tree

Their run-and-gun style put them on as many as 15 bucks in a single day—way more than the average Sonora hunter sees in an entire week.

line with a good view of small openings on the cross- and downwind sides. Unbelievably, he pulled out a little mouth call and commenced blowin'.

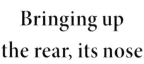

Bringing up the rear, its nose

One of many call sites at which the author almost pulled the trigger. He saw tempting bucks every single day of his hunt.

buried in the rear end of a comely doe, was the biggest typical mule deer I've ever seen on the hoof.

He called for a solid 10 minutes, alternately glassing the brush off to our sides. I had already put down my binocular and shoved my freezing

hands into my pockets when the first buck came trotting into view. It came in from our right at a fast gait and was on our downwind side quickly. My client readied his rifle while I put my binocular on the buck and hit the rangefinder. At 104 yards, the buck stopped directly downwind in the shade of a spindly tree and stared at us, neither curious nor scared. Rather, it seemed to be looking over, under, around and through us as it

searched for the source of the pained, pitiful wailing that had attracted it.

Troy and I quickly dismissed the buck as a youngish, 170-class deer. It stayed there another four or five minutes until Troy finished calling, climbed down and drove away. As we drove on to the next spot, my buddy and I jabbered excitedly about the confidence and ease with which Troy called in that buck. According to Troy, the fawn-in-distress call fools bucks into thinking a doe had just kicked her fawn off because she was coming into estrus—a deadly prerut tactic.

That day and all of the next, we witnessed Troy call in deer after deer. There were a few spots that didn't pan out, but we were batting well over 50 percent. Many of the bucks were

smaller, but we saw some big boys, too. Besides, it was nice to see so many deer in an area where most outfitters consider it a good hunt when they show their clients three or four bucks in a week.

The most impressive buck we saw on day two was pushing 40 inches wide with tremendous mass. It was one of seven bucks that responded almost immediately to the call. They came from different directions, but they all converged on the same small opening. They stood there and watched us for at least five minutes, so we had plenty of time to look them over. Unfortunately, as wide and massive as the big boy was, his tines were short and he was only a 3x4. My buddy and I both thought long and hard about shooting him, but it was early in the hunt and that wasn't the deer we'd come all the way to Mexico for.

We called in several deer on day three, but high winds kept the call from carrying far and, we assumed, had the deer hunkered down in their beds. It turned out to be the slowest day of the hunt, but it ended in exciting fashion.

We had just finished calling and were headed back to the house when a big group of deer crossed the ranch road in front of us. Bringing up the rear, its nose buried in the rear end of a comely doe, was the biggest typical mule deer I've ever seen on the hoof. Its massive, boxy rack towered above its head, and its deep forks and wrist-thick beams added greatly to the dramatic effect that monstrous rack had on us all. Though only 25 or 26 inches wide, the massive 4x4 rack was easily more than 200 inches. Unfortunately, his girlfriend

When the author's friend wounded a monster mulie, they hired cowboys with horses and dogs to try and find it.

was on the move, and he wasn't about to let her out of his sight. We hopped out and followed on foot, but we ran out of shooting light before we could catch them.

That night we relived the deer sighting time and again. By now, Hunter had joined us in camp and was busy taunting and teasing me for doubting him all those months. Despite his smack-talk, he and Troy were as excited as we were by that bruiser. We sat around the fireplace late into the night trying to formulate a good plan for taking the once-in-a-lifetime buck.

We didn't spook the group the night before, so we decided to go back the next morning to try and call him in. We knew the odds were slim

that a rutting buck would leave a hot doe to respond to our call, but it was a damn big buck and we were willing to try just about anything. Despite our good-natured ribbing and optimistic banter, when we rolled out of camp that morning I don't think any of us really thought we had the slightest chance of finding that buck.

We'd seen the group near a tank the night before. Lacking any better ideas, we parked a quarter mile away from the pond and slipped in, then set up in some low brush atop the earthen dam. After allowing a few minutes for everything to settle, Troy whipped out his call and started trying to work his magic.

He called hard for a solid 10 or 15 minutes, but not a single buck showed itself. Still, we wanted that buck to be in the area so badly that we sat tight and scanned the brush while Troy called until he just couldn't call anymore. He had just put down the call when a dark, stocky buck came charging toward us. When it cleared the brush, there was no doubt that it was the same towering, heavy-horned hombre we'd seen the night before. It had obviously come a long way, because its mouth was wide open and he looked plum tuckered, but he was practically in our laps when he skidded to a stop under a small tree.

My client's rifle was already on the sticks, so Troy and I both hissed,

CALLING MULE DEER

My guides weren't too forthcoming with mule deer calling tips. In fact, they were downright secretive. The only thing they were open about was why bucks respond to their fawn bleats. According to them, the main reason bucks respond is that they think the sound is emanating from a fawn that has just been kicked off by its mother when she comes into estrus. The amorous bucks come hard and fast to be the first to find those wanton does.

Their other theory is that bucks come because they know does will respond to any fawn in distress. This certainly proved true on my hunt, as multiple does responded almost every time we called. Regardless of why they respond, calling can be effective from the prerut all the way to the end of the season.

Figuring out the basics of calling mulies wasn't all that tough. The guys didn't vocalize much of what they were doing on my hunt, but I've been calling and rattling whitetails for years.

You might think the call you choose is important, but Hunter Ross and Troy Calaway have similar success with totally different calls. Hunter uses a stock call, while Troy customized his call a bit to give him the plaintive, pitiful tone he likes. On a recent Colorado mule deer hunt, my guide used a common rabbit-in-distress call to mimic the sound of a distressed fawn.

Whether you choose the True Talker 2 from Hunter Specialties (hunterspecialties.com), Primos' Hardwood Fawn Bleat (primos.com) or Knight & Hale's Double Reed Fawn Bleat (knightandhale.com), the key is to sound as pitiful as possible and choose a set-up that forces bucks to cross some open ground as they work to get downwind of your position. My guides called for as long as 20 minutes at most set-ups with a few two- or three-minute breaks in the calling sequence.

Don't expect to master mule deer calling by reading this sidebar, but these basics are a great place to start.

---

simply, "Shoot!" The buck was almost broadside, and the distance was less than 100 yards. It looked like a gimme for my buddy, who is a damn fine shot and a very experienced hunter, but stuff happens when you go from zero to 100 miles per hour in the blink of an eye and add more than 200 inches of antlers to the equation. Even so, I was shocked when I saw the buck take the bullet low and way too far back.

We spent all that day and half of the next one looking for that buck. We hired cowboys to ride the brush on horses, and we walked ourselves silly scouring every inch of brush we could cover, but we never did find him. My friend retreated into some dark, quiet place while we did our best to regroup after the crushing loss.

Day five, I went looking for a buck of my own. We called a few spots, but all we saw were young bucks. On a whim, we drove toward a section of the ranch we hadn't hunted much in hopes of changing our luck. Shortly, we spotted a high, wide brute chasing a doe across a clearing.

I bailed out and trotted off in hopes of intercepting the buck, but I didn't have to go far. The doe wasn't the least bit interested in spending quality time in the brush with her amorous admirer, so she cut back and started trotting right toward me with the big buck on her tail. At 125 yards, he turned, giving me an easy chest-on shot. I noticed something a bit odd about his rack, but it was high and wide, so I plastered the reticle low on the buck's chest and sent a 180-grain Tipped Trophy Bonded Bear Claw from my .300 WSM on its way.

The buck buckled at the shot, but quickly gained his footing and made

a hard U-turn. I immediately sent another big slug toward his heart, Texas style, which dropped the wide-racked buck in his tracks. I was ecstatic, but I had to take a minute to let the king-size shot of adrenaline work its way through my system before I could walk over and see my deer.

As I approached him, I couldn't fathom what I'd seen about his rack that was off. Even from 100 yards it was easy to see that the rack was wide and heavy. I figured it would score in the high 190s if everything was intact, but as I got closer I saw

the problem. Though the buck's frame was as big as I thought, its rack lacked back forks. The deer looked exactly like a typical eight-point whitetail on steroids. Its inside spread was 28¾ inches, and it scored over 178. With good forks, it would have easily gone over 190, but I wasn't complaining. It was a hell of a buck and a great way to end the most fun and exciting mule deer hunt I've ever experienced.

Back in camp, Hunter had much to be proud of. In addition to my big buck, another client of mine, Kent Hall, had just come in with a wide,

heavy buck that scored almost 190 inches. Hunter was also feeling pretty smug because, in his opinion, he had put an end to all my doubts about his calling ability. I, of course, reminded him that night that it was Troy who had done all the calling. Sure, Hunter had called in plenty of bucks for my other client, but if it will get me a return invitation, I'm not about to give him credit for those.

Greg hunted with Hunter Ross of Desert Safaris —desertsafaris.com. Ⓗ

NEW BRUNSWICK BEAR

2010
NON RESIDENT
NON-RÉSIDENT
165110
IF TAG IS DETACHED
LICENCE IS
VOID
FOR BEAR HUNTING
BUT MUST BE
DETACHED TO

REDUX

WORDS & IMAGES by
MIKE SCHOBY

SOME SAY
"THIRD TIME'S THE CHARM."

SOMETIMES IT
ONLY TAKES TWICE.

As I squashed the 497th New Brunswick mosquito between my thumb and finger, two thoughts ran through my mind. First, I needed to remember to bring my ThermaCELL, and second, I wished that loudmouth from the Fredericton bar who said that "Killing bears over bait was unsporting" was sitting beside me.

On the shelves you will find everything from dusty boxes of .30-30 cartridges to baking powder to Dutch ovens and steel traps. The walls are covered with mahogany-colored heavy deer racks and tattered, faded photos of hunters with 300-pound whitetails, gigantic bears, piles of coyotes and stringers of fish.

**I**N FOUR DAYS I hadn't seen so much as a cub on a bait. What was sporting was the biblical downpours, clouds of starving mosquitoes and a wet cold that soaked into the bones. So much for baited bear being easy.

This was my second trip to New Brunswick. Both times I hunted with Charles Lindsay of Lindsay Sporting Camps (lindsaysportingcamps. com). My first bear hunt with him yielded no bear, which was no one's fault but my own. Charles did his homework and had many active baits going. I just didn't spend enough time hunting. Pressing work issues forced me to return home after just a couple of days. I left the boreal wonderland and vowed to return. The province is gorgeous, and I knew that it was loaded with bears. I just needed to spend more time in-country to make it happen.

HUNTING IN BLACK AND WHITE

There is something about New Brunswick that harks to another era, a time when the words "North Woods"

The general store in Millville had everything from steel traps to Tampax. While feminine hygiene products are not usually associated with a bear hunt, when you run out of wicks to pour bear attractant scent onto, they make a decent substitute.

were said in a low, reverent tone. It's a place of adventure, deep timber and big game. Looking at the landscape and the surrounding towns, you can picture everything in black and white. Take for example the general store in Millville. On the shelves you will find everything from dusty boxes of .30-30 cartridges to baking powder to Dutch ovens and steel traps. The walls are covered with mahogany-colored heavy deer racks and tattered, faded photos of hunters with 300-pound whitetails, gigantic bears, piles of coyotes and stringers of fish. The country hasn't changed much since Charles Lindsay's grandfather first opened this camp for affluent eastern sportsmen nearly a century ago.

It was with this sense of place that I selected a rifle for the hunt. I felt that a lever gun would be fitting, but a traditional blued and walnut lever action would be even better, something that looked and felt like an original Winchester Model 94 but with modern improvements that made it more effective. After doing some research, I decided that a Mossberg 464 in .30-30 fit the bill to a "T." It's available in two versions, straight grip or pistol grip, and I selected the latter. It measured 6¾ pounds and 38½ inches. I liked the way it balanced in my hands, and the short overall length would make it extremely handy in the tight woods of New Brunswick.

When my individual rifle arrived, I was shocked at the quality of the walnut. Not only was it better than any other lever gun I own, I believe it is better than any rifle or shotgun I own, period. And that is saying something. The quality of the walnut on the Mossberg 464 is something

hunters and shooters have not seen in the last 50 years, and the deep, rich blueing heralds the look of a bygone era.

After the carressing period was over, I took it to the range and quickly discovered that its beauty wasn't just skin deep. The rifle shot very well. The 20-inch button-rifled barrel with its recessed target crown lives up to the company's commitment to accuracy across the Mossberg line, centerfire or rimfire alike. In addition to the quality barrel, I believe the unique action with the well-thought-out bolt ensures solid lockup and helps contribute to the superb accuracy.

I ran some Hornady and Federal ammunition through it and saw extremely good groups—cloverleaves at 50 yards that stayed just over an inch at 100 yards. Now, keep in mind that I scoped the rifle—my eyes won't do that well with iron sights anymore (not that they likely ever would have, but with age, lying about how good you used to be gets easier). And while a scope is not completely traditional, sometimes function needs to prevail over form. It's a combination of classic lines and new technology. The Mossberg 464 is set up from the factory to easily mount a scope, and once it's there, it performs flawlessly. In addition to the drilled and tapped receiver, the hammer spur has a threaded hole to readily accept a side spur for easier cocking when a scope is mounted—another well-thought-out feature.

ANOTHER NIGHT ON STAND

With Charles in the driver's seat, we headed out for the evening hunt. When we arrived at the stand, the bait was being actively hit and the day was

Once the decision is made to hunt with a traditional, classic rifle, other like choices follow suit. An American-made Redfield scope, Filson jacket and Filson luggage complete the outfit.

beautiful. The tree stand was tucked deep in an evergreen forest overlooking a sun-lit natural opening. I was mosquito-free, since I remembered to bring my ThermaCELL, and the night was devoid of rain. As wonderful an evening as it was, it was also devoid of bears. Luckily, my bear-less situation was an isolated event, and even as I watched the sun dip toward the horizon, my buddy Tom Taylor was being overrun by bears a couple of miles away. With light fading, he shot his first black bear, also with a Mossberg 464. That night around camp was a happy one that yielded many stories as memories were relived.

THE LAST NIGHT

As I headed afield the last night of the hunt, I could hardly believe that

In New Brunswick, like much of Canada, bears are hunted over bait. In addition to natural food, successful hunters often use scents such as Wildlife Research Center's Ultimate Bear Lure.

a week had passed so quickly and that I was facing the very real chance that I would be heading back from New Brunswick for a second time sans bear. As we drove to a new stand, Charles assured me that this was the hottest bait he had, with multiple bears being seen on it every night. According to him, this stand had lots of bears, big bears, and most seemed to be suffering from a mental deficiency. In short, the setup sounded perfect, but I wasn't holding my breath. If something is a 99 percent sure thing, I seem to often fall into the 1 percent crowd.

Within a few minutes of being dropped off, I walked into the woods, climbed into a stand and was just getting settled for a long evening wait when I heard a small twig snap. It wasn't much past 4 p.m.—too early for a bear to come in—when I caught movement in the brush. A few seconds passed, and a bear appeared. Broad daylight, no rain, and I hadn't

even squashed my first mosquito. Showing just a bit of caution, the bear came out, knocked over the bait barrel, grabbed a hunk of meat and ran off. Instead of running back the way he came, he ran right toward me, stopping to eat the meat directly under my stand. As he chewed away, another bear emerged from the timber and sauntered into the bait. This one was bigger and showed no trepidation. I figured that, for a last-night's bear, he was big enough. Even with four more hours until dark, I decided not to risk going home empty-handed and quietly cocked back the hammer. The bear was quartering away, and after two years of hunting, I let the hammer fall. He dropped at the shot and didn't twitch. I levered the remaining shells out of the rifle and climbed down out of my stand, my New Brunswick bear quest coming to a close.

The relief in Charles' voice was evident when I radioed him five

minutes later. Being that it was the last night of the hunt, it was a fitting end. We had plenty of daylight left to skin the bear and prep the hide for transport the next day. It wasn't the largest bear I have ever shot, or the largest that Charles' clients took that season, but it was a good bear and one that I had paid for in time, mosquito bites and rain. While I would have loved to have hung my tag on a coal-black Boone & Crockett giant, there is a large part of me that is glad I didn't. It gives me a reason to go back to New Brunswick. I am already anticipating the North Woods, the historic towns and, in a strange way, even the mosquitoes. While hunting always has its uncertainties, you can rest assured that one thing will be certain: I will visit the northern wonderland of New Brunswick again. Ⓗ

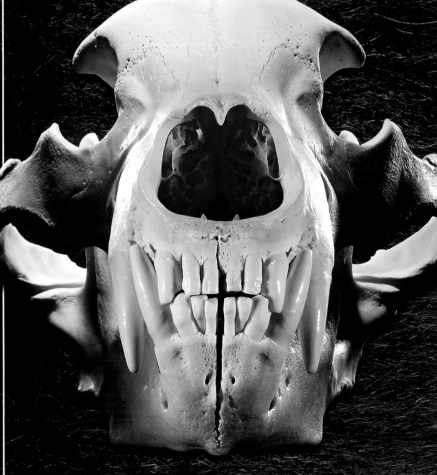

BLACK
MAGIC

MIKE SCHOBY • CRAIG BODDINGTON

SKIP KNOWLES • DOUG HOWLETT

YOUR GUIDE TO THE ADDICTIVE VOODOO OF BLACK BEAR HUNTING, FROM GUNS AND GEAR TO TROPHY HOT SPOTS AND CULINARY DELIGHTS.

What a democracy we live in, where any hunter who can raise a gun has access to a reasonably priced black bear tag and public land to chase them. In fact, pursuit of happiness for more and more of us translates to pursuit of *Ursus americanus*, the aptly named all-American everyman's dangerous game. Bear numbers are booming across the nation, from Florida and Jersey all the way to Oregon, and nonresident tags are dirt cheap compared with other big-game species and often over-the-counter. They're the smartest and toughest North American game animal, and widely distributed. But what bears really do is put the adventure back in hunting, the goosebumps, the chills, the mystery and hint of danger that come with chasing critters that occasionally eat people. They're unpredictable in more ways than one. Shoot two bears off a given bait and one will pile up within 20 feet from a well-placed arrow and the next will run for miles shot end-to-end with a 12-gauge slug. And there's an undeniable spookiness about bears that is unnerving, to say the least. They move more silently than any other big game, carefully stepping in their own footprints on approach paths to a bait, appearing like black smoke through the trees. You feel safe in that tree until a monster walks out, turns his massive head and stares straight at you. *Oh yeah, they can climb trees.* And can they ever! When they really want to, they don't shimmy up trees, they bound straight up them in leaps. A wounded bear will use its paws to pack mud into its wounds. Cre-e-e-epy. Grown men have literally loaded their pants when bluff-charged. You don't get *that* on a deer hunt. If you have yet to pursue what might be this nation's greatest game animal, it's time to man up and plan a rendezvous with a big boar black bear. Besides, it's a great way to justify a new rifle. Over these seven pages, we'll tell you all you need to know to get going.

Dream BEAR GUNS

SINCE BEARS are hunted across a vast array of terrain and by widely varied methods, picking a single "ideal" bear gun is next to impossible. But if we were allowed to narrow it down to just a few, these would be our picks...

HOUND HUNTING PARTNER

It is Newton's 27th law of physics: After a couple of miles of chasing a pack of hounds through the mountains, every ounce becomes a pound. And when the hounds have finally done their work and brought old blackie to bay, the shot is generally stationery and no farther than the tallest tree. A long-range rifle is not required, so why carry it? Slide an S&W 329PD into a Galco holster and head afield instead. At 2 ½ pounds fully loaded with .44 Magnum hunting cartridges and leather holster, this is all the medicine you will need for a treed bruin. — *smith-wesson.com*

ALASKA BROWNIE BRAWLER

When going for the biggest bears in the world in arguably the harshest environment known to man, a rifle often needs to step up to the plate. In the search for the ideal brown bear rifle, the Kimber 8400 Talkeetna fills the bill. Not only is this stainless steel, Kevlar-stocked rifle built to stand up to an Alaskan heavyweight-style pounding, it only tips the scales as a welterweight. Weighing in around eight pounds, this well-balanced, lightweight (for caliber) rifle is ideal for trudging mile after mile through the bogs, tundra and mountains of Alaska. Available in .375 H&H, this rifle packs enough punch for even the largest of brown bears. —*kimberamerica.com*

SPOT AND STALK PERFECTION

Savage's recently introduced Bear Hunter model takes the trusted 116 to the next level. Anytime you combine an Accutrigger and a camo Accustock with a stainless-barreled action, you have a heck of a combination. Available in .338 Win. Mag., .300 Win. Mag., .300 WSM and .325 WSM in two action lengths, this rifle has "western" and "Alaskan bear hunting" written all over it. As an ear-saving bonus, the Bear Hunter comes from the factory with an adjustable on/off muzzlebrake. Saving your shoulder at the range as well as your buddy's ears in the field has never been so easy.
—*savagearms.com*

NOSTALGIC CLASS

Some hunters choose the look, feel and quality of a rifle over numerical, quantifiable performance data. Luckily, dual-minded individuals who value function as well as form no longer have to choose. Turnbull Manufacturing Company offers ex-

BEAR FACTS: Total black bear populations across North America are believed to be between 600,000 to 700,000 animals. A male bear has a territory of around 12,000 acres. A sow has a territory that stretches over 6,000 acres.

quisite modern 1886 Winchesters in period grace, elegance and class (and several grades) in the modern .475 Turnbull caliber. Pushing a 400-grain bullet at 2,150 fps to produce 4,104 ft-lbs of energy, the .475 Turnbull is big medicine for black bears, grizzly and brownies alike. So if silky-smooth actions, dripping-wet color case-hardening and walnut that looks like it grew around metal are your thing (if not, please stop reading this immediately and see a psychologist), your prayers have been answered.
—*turnbullmfg.com*

BLACK GUNS, BLACK BEARS

For hunters looking for a modern sporting rifle to fill the role of bear gun, few do it better than the Rock River Arms .458 SOCOM. Short, compact and packing plenty of punch, think of the .458 SOCOM as a .45-70 round specifically tailored to fit into a standard AR-15 magazine and frame. While there is a wide variety of bullet weights and velocities, the standard 300-grainer going around 2,000 fps is more than enough for blackies on bait, up a tree or even 150 yards away across a clearing. If you don't own an AR and want one to hunt with, this is a great choice. If you already own one in .223, simply buy the upper assembly from Rock River and head for the woods. Keep in mind that this rifle is not the one to take to Canada—we've had several reports that ARs are a problem at the border.
—*rockriverarms.com*

ULTIMATE BEAR HUNTS

Thanks to the widespread black bear, North America has the lion's share of the world's bear-hunting opportunities, but the bear family is actually widespread, with members occurring in South America and across Eurasia. Many varieties are depleted and properly protected today, so the primary opportunity for bear hunting outside North America lies with *Ursus arctos*, the good old grizzly bear.

Technically called the Eurasian brown bear, the humpbacked, long-clawed, dish-faced bear is found discontinuously from the Spanish Pyrenees to the great expanse of Russia and Central Asia. Current hunting opportunities are limited across this vast range, but there are some very interesting bear hunts in the Old World.

Perhaps the very best opportunity is in Russia, where bears are widespread and the population is generally healthy. A traditional Russian hunting technique is called "bear in the den," conducted in winter and early spring. In this insane gambit, the hunters find a denned bear, wake him up and take him when, justifiably enraged, he charges out of the den.

In coastal Siberia and especially the Kamchatka Peninsula, the brown bears are similar to Alaskan brown bears. I think the best Alaskan bears grow bigger, but the average in Kamchatka exceeds Alaska. If a guy wanted to take just one "coastal brown bear," I would probably recommend Kamchatka. Hunting with a mixture of cross-country skis and snowshoes, I shot a wonderful bear there when Russia first opened back in 1991. That was a great adventure then; today bear hunting in Kamchatka has developed into a great hunting program that remains well organized and highly successful.

Opportunities are much more limited in Europe, with a small harvest in Scandinavia and scattered permits across Eastern Europe. Without question, the very best opportunity lies in Romania, where the majority of Europe's brown bears reside and have perhaps the most dense population in the world. The traditional technique is driving, but as permits become fewer this is becoming less common because hunting over bait is much more selective. —*CB*

BIG BEARS

When it comes to sizing bears, the yardstick varies by region. In some places hunters use live weigh. However, this is often fraught with challenges, as some bears are gutted, some are skinned and other times folks just don't have a scale handy so they resort to estimation...hence there are a lot more "500 pounders" than "200 pounders" (in reality, for every 500-pound bear shot, there are dozens of 200-pound bears taken). In other regions, the measurement in feet is the benchmark of a trophy. A bear taping seven feet from tail to nose is called a "seven footer." For black bears, anything over six feet in most places is considered a shooter; tack on a foot for southeast Alaska and Vancouver Island.

But the only method recognized by Boone & Crockett (boone-crockett. org) is skull size. The good news is that it's so simple, even *HUNTING* editors can figure it out. With calipers, measure from the front to the back of the skull (lower jaw removed), then from side to side. Add the two measurements together and voilá, you have the bear's score. An average black bear in the lower 48 will be somewhere between 16 and 18 inches, but exceptional bears will measure between 19 and 21. To make the Boone & Crockett record book, the minimum size is 20 inches for the awards book, 21 inches for the all-time book. The largest black bear of all time recorded with Boone & Crockett was a "picked up" skull from Utah that measured 23 ⁹⁄₁₆ —MS

FIELD*JUDGING*

Of all big-game animals in North America, bears are among the toughest to judge in the field and for first-timers—all bears, even yearlings, look huge. A few tricks from noted New Brunswick bear guide Charles Lindsay (lindsaysportingcamps.com) help clue in hunters. "Look at the body first. A truly big bear carries himself differently than a younger, immature bear. They will have a swayed back, large gut, splayed legs and little daylight between the belly and the ground." In addition to physical characteristics, try to judge his attitude. Lindsay continues, "A b[ig] bear has an air of dominance an[d] surety surrounding him when h[e] comes into a bait." After the body an[d] attitude, turn to the noggin as a[n] indicator. A large bear's head w[ill] appear blocky with ears that are sm[all] and spaced far apart. Spend plen[ty] of time looking a bear over befo[re] pulling the trigger, as mistakes a[re] common and many a hunter ha[s] radioed back to camp reporting "th[e] new world record" he just shot, on[ly] to walk up and discover the be[ar] somehow shrank considerably. —[?]

Wisconsin has the most Boone & Crockett record black bear entries of all time with 402.

BEAR FACTS: Between 1900 and 1980, black bears killed 23 people. There have been 19 such fatal attacks in

LOADED

FOR BEAR

When it comes to loads for bears, bigger is often better. Yes, bears can be killed with small calibers, but shot placement is critical. Most hunters typically opt for calibers such as the .30-06, .300 WSM and .338 Federal. As for bullets, a hunter wants to go with something that holds together when hitting bone and offers good controlled expansion.

"An ideal black bear bullet is very similar to an ideal whitetail bullet, but it should exhibit more controlled expansion," says Mike Stock, centerfire product manager at Winchester. "The value of exit holes is hotly debated among black bear hunters because of the difficulty in blood-tracking bears due to the high fat concentration that closes up entry and exit holes." Use a bullet built for maximum internal damage, plant it well, and a bear won't go far.

Among Winchester's line, good bullet choices are Ballistic Silvertips or Power Max Bonded. Great options from Federal are the Trophy Bonded Tip and Fusion, while Nosler Partitions or AccuBonds, Remington Core-Lokt and Hornady InterBond or GMX also deliver great black bear performance. For deep-penetrating choices in lever guns and revolvers, take a look at Buffalo Bore's offerings. They use hardcast lead bullets not designed to expand but to penetrate, punching a full-bore hole all the way through the body with a large exit hole. —DH

JURASSIC BRUINS

So you want a trophy black bear? One with a luxurious black coat sans rub marks, huge paws and the magical 21 inches of bone between the ears…it's every bear hunter's dream. But where to go? Alberta and Manitoba are good choices; Vancouver Island, British Columbia, is another terrific bet; and if you can pull a tag, Wisconsin is a top choice. However, year after year it's pretty tough to beat Prince of Wales Island (POW, as it's called locally) in Southeast Alaska. Like Vancouver Island, POW is inhabited by extremely large bears that have the food, genetics and lifespan to frequently make the book. According to Brad Saalsaa, noted POW bear guide (weguidealaska.com), "While it may not be as good as it was a decade ago before it was 'discovered,' [POW] is still a darn good place to hunt trophy bears. Best of all, we hunt them in a unique manner." While baiting is legal on POW, Saalsaa and his crew tout the island as the place to spot and stalk bears. After a hunt I did with them several years ago, I have to agree. In the course of a single evening, spotting a dozen or so bruisers cruising the coastline and surrounding mountains is a relatively common occurrence. But with so many bears, hunters tend to get picky, passing up bears that are considered shooters anywhere else in the world. However, once the right bear is found, hunters plot a course to ambush it or they put on a sneak. Sometimes a bear-skin rug is at the end of the adventure, while other times fate throws a curve ball. Either way, for ADD hunters like myself, it beats the heck out of sitting over a bait pile swatting mosquitoes. —MS

SPOT & STALK BLACK BEARS

Alberta is a forgiving place for a bear hunter. With off-the-hook bear densities, it's one of the few places that allow hunters to take two bears. Success rates are virtually 100 percent for hunters getting their first bear, and they don't drop much for the second. After filling both tags hunting over bait with Alberta Bear Busters in 2009, I decided to try spot and stalk when I returned in 2010 to hunt with Red Willow Outfitters.

Alberta's long, remote gas line and logging roads make for a Texas-style spot and stalk (plenty of driving), and before my hunt was over, I would cover my fair share of ground via truck, ATV and, ultimately, boot leather.

"At this time of year, bears get to feeding and don't look up too much," says Red Willow Outfitters owner Todd Loewen. "If the wind is right and you have trees to hide behind as you work closer, you can get right in on a bear." But that wind had better be right.

With the Browning X-bolt in .30-06, I decided I'd like to get to within 150 yards since the point was still to stalk the bear and not just put the long-distance smackdown on one.

Riding and looking down side roads for roaming bears, we spotted a cinnamon one about 400 yards away. With grizzlies in the area, we weren't 100 percent sure that this wasn't one.

The previous year, I had passed up a color-phase bear my first night on the stand. I wasn't sure that it was big enough. I wrongly assumed the bear hit the bait every night and I would have another chance—as it turned out, he didn't.

Now was my chance for redemption. With the wind at our back, my guide and I slipped to within 100 yards of the bear. I eased into the open dirt road to gain an un-obstructed shot, waited for the bear to move—a definite brown-colored bruin—and made a perfect lung shot. The bear dashed 30 yards before collapsing into an expanse of foot-deep water. Redemption was mine.

Before the hunt was over, I would pass up another two dozen bears and have the wind foil another stalk on a black bear so big it looked like Sasquatch doubled over after a night of drinking. We got to within 160 yards when suddenly I felt the wind on the back of my neck. I looked up, and like a ghost, the bruin disappeared into the province's dark, alluring forest. —*DH*

A 3.5 ounce piece of bear meat contains 8.3 grams of fat and 20.1 grams of protein.

AWESOME D.I.Y. HUNTS

It's a gut-clenching thrill to be glassing alpine country for mule deer, your brain keyed up for antlers and ears, and suddenly spot a great big black bear in front of you. Even more so when you have a bear tag in your pocket. It's happening more than ever in the Pacific Northwest, where hound bans have resulted in a bear boom to create one of the best values in nonresident big-game hunts. Growing up in Washington in the '80s, I didn't think shooting black bears was a big deal. I lucked into three bear kills on public before I ever even went bear hunting! All were incidental to deer hunting, and tags were over-the-counter and cheap. Color-phase bears were common, too. The first was a blond, the second a big cinnamon that remains one of my favorite hunting memories with my old man. I am happy to say that even in the good-old-days-oriented world of hunting, for once, Northwest bear hunting is better than ever. Due to hound bans, some states have reinstated spring seasons. And in Idaho, dogs and bait are legal, but spiraling wolf numbers keep houndsmen from running bears because wolves kill bear dogs like coyotes eat housecats. Most states now have a two-bear limit to boost harvest, and some type of bear season runs nearly half the year. The best part? In Washington, nonresident bear/cougar combo tags cost only $242, about half a deer tag. And once you find that way-outta-the-way berry patch, you can return annually with great success. The high country of the Cascades and NE Washington is best, with the nation's highest bear densities, and early September is prime. Lush and brushy, Western Washington is tougher because of the foliage, but bear-infested. The best bet here is to glass alpine western slopes of the Cascades or hunt timberland clearcuts. In Idaho, baiting is legal but complicated. Skip it, and scour the logging roads in the panhandle as they green up in spring, and glass the region's dense huckleberry patches in fall. Moving to Utah 12 years ago, I found that bear hunting is in fact a pretty big deal outside the Northwest, with tough limited entry regs. I miss wandering that high Northwest country, looking for big bears and mulies at the same time. It's still completely doable and affordable. —*SK*

MAN eating BEAR?

As much as hunters live in fear of feeling bear teeth sink in their rear end, truth is we eat a lot more of them than vice versa each year. Most guys just make sausage, sausage and more sausage out of their bear, because with enough pork fat and spice you can make road-killed possum a culinary delight. But there are other ways. I've heard of chefs paying outlandish sums for bear meat (exoticmeatsandmore.com lists it at $165 for 3 1/2 pounds of leg meat!), so think about that next time you snub bear steaks. I've had it many ways, but the only way I've truly loved it was corned, in which case the steaks were delicious and tender, helped by the fact that I was dirt poor at the time. Find someone who can corn meat, preferably a mad Irish butcher, and you are in for a lifetime of guilt-free bear hunting. Better still, do it yourself (go to ehow.com and search "how to make corned beef"). Not too difficult and way worth it. —SK

BEAR with US

The problem with bears is that you can't just cut off their horns. Sure, they're among the all-time top game animals, but they are a cumbersome trophy once downed. A big furry blob, hard to move, sliding around in their skin like a raccoon. With deer, it's simple. Is this my biggest one ever, and so will it be a shoulder mount or Euro-mount? But with bears, there's no simple resolution. Out of respect for the animal, you have to do something with that hide, even if it's your tenth one, and bored taxidermists' attempts to get wildly creative with stuffed bears can backfire. At Safari Club International's show in Reno this year, there were hundreds of bears, most of it pretty neat stuff: fighting bears, bears downing deer, etc. Then there were...the others. Stuff that is fun to see, but gives you pause. Like a large cub lying on its back, holding up a glass table with its feet. Cool! Except . . . wait a minute, somebody has to explain why they shot this baby bear, or, in some cases, entire families of bears (a surprisingly frequent display). And other mounts, like one of a smiling bear sprawled out on a limb with a butterfly on its nose, Disney style, just create way

Photo Credit: animalartistry.com

Bear taxidermy comes in all forms from comical, to amazing like this piece by Animal Artistry.

too much sympathy for the animal, though the ever-popular ferociously snarling bear shoulder mount is arguably as ridiculous, considering most bears die with a mouth full of berries. If the mount doesn't make you cringe, that price tag will. What we need is a $50 do-it-yourself bear tanning kit. A recent Canada bear trip left me holding a bill for over $600 just to have one tanned, not even as a rug. *HUNTING'S* staff mostly tans ours (Moyle Mink & Tannery moytown.com does a good job at a great price) instead of getting them rugged. It's cheaper, and you're not going to break your toe or spill your Scotch by stumbling over a large, protruding skull in the middle of your living room in the dark (or start a war with the neighbors when their dog chews three claws off your $800 rug). Problem is, even big,— sixfoot-plus bears shrink a good bit when not stretched properly for a rug, and improper tanning yields a black, coyote-sized throw rug when it's done, which is demoralizing. Might as well be a cub-coffee table. Seems nothing about this bear hunting business is easy, and that is probably as it should be. —SK ⓗ

KODIAK, OR KARDIAK?
Chasing DIY Sitka blacktail on an island where you are not at the top of the food chain.

WELCOME TO THE

WORDS & IMAGES by
SKIP KNOWLES

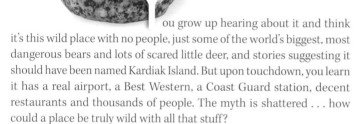

You grow up hearing about it and think it's this wild place with no people, just some of the world's biggest, most dangerous bears and lots of scared little deer, and stories suggesting it should have been named Kardiak Island. But upon touchdown, you learn it has a real airport, a Best Western, a Coast Guard station, decent restaurants and thousands of people. The myth is shattered . . . how could a place be truly wild with all that stuff?

Step about 50 yards into the bush, that oh-so-dense and dark wet brush, and you find out in a hurry why Kodiak Island is still called The Rock.

"The brown bear threat is greatly overhyped," said the men running the *Sundy*, our 56-foot floating base camp. "They don't come running to the gunshots like everyone says," they told me. "Few real problems," they promised.

I hit the beach the first morning with Len Nelson–two Kodiak virgins with no guide–and we hunted along the sand and rock shoreline probably 30 minutes, admiring huge bear tracks, before cutting inland through a thicket to a small rise overlooking the thicket, which now lay between us and shore. And just like that, your months of pre-trip fears are realized.

"Brooowwwwrrr, rowwrr-oggh-oggh-oggh-oggh-oggh!"

The unmistakable sound of a very large, very angry animal, very close, from the thicket below. It sounded like a lion's roar segueing into an outboard's propeller chopping thick mud after running aground, or a V8 with a blown exhaust manifold missing on two cylinders. Except cars with bad exhaust don't leap from the brush to tear your throat out.

"What was that!?" Len said urgently, hunching behind his .300 Win. Mag.

R·O·C·K

"I'd say by the way you're holding that rifle you know exactly what *that* was," I said to him, leaning forward, my gun raised. It sounded like the prelude to a charge, a warning, maybe 50 yards away. I walked to the edge of the ledge in front of us above the thicket so I could see more. If he was coming, I wanted to get a shot before he suddenly popped up 12 feet away.

For emphasis, again, from the thicket: *"Broowow-ow-oowow-grroowwrr."*

You don't have to tell us three times. We got the hell out of there, walking back-to-back, moving through dark blowdowns. The only sound was rain and wind, but we "heard the footsteps" all day long. I started glassing from a cliff an hour later and turned to see Len with his back to me, covering the woods behind us. We did not like being backed against the cliff, and left. We agreed not to shoot a buck unless it was a monster, knowing we would probably never get a deer out of this spot, based on all we'd heard.

The Rock has always been a harsh place. Russian fur traders took over in the 18th century, enslaving the Aleuts and killing off 85 percent of them, forcing the natives to hunt the sea

"YOU NEVER KNOW WHERE THE BASTARDS ARE GONNA BE." HE WASN'T TALKING ABOUT THE DEER.

otters they revered to near extinction (the otters are everywhere today). In 1941 a fort was built to fight the Japanese, and in 1964, just five years after statehood, the Alaska Earthquake sent tsunamis 30 feet high to the

island, killing 15 people and destroying the fishing fleets and Standard Oil. The Navy SEALs train here at a special cold-weather warfare detachment. The weather is famously savage.

And I'd heard plenty about the bears. Five feet high at the shoulder, males averaging just over 1,000 pounds, and an unbelievable population density of a bear every .7 square miles! Tyler Meinhold, a guide friend who knows what it's like to kill an attacking record-book grizzly at 15 feet with a 12 gauge (and have the gun jam), told me to bring a big rifle, don't fight bears for deer and that the island is infested with them. "You may have trouble finding a brown on the mainland, but not Kodiak," he assured. The leader of our trip, Doug Jeanneret, of US Sportsmen's Alliance, admitted that they'd had conflicts in past trips, including a guy who had to shoot a sow that stalked them repeatedly. A pair of Doug's hunters had a bear

circle and steal a deer from them WHILE they were dragging it, pulling it right from their hands.

On the plane ride in I met an accountant who hunts tribal land because he works for native corporations, and he said, "We call it The Rock because it's all by itself way out there in the middle of nowhere, and the weather just slams it uninterrupted by terrain.

"You've never been, huh? It's a beautiful place, big mountains, huge views, lots of lakes and bays, tons of fish and wildlife, a wild place, so pretty, but it just gets blasted by Mother Nature. I hope you get the good Kodiak, 40 degrees, blue skies; it can really be amazing. But lots of search and rescues out there."

He'd just returned from an early high-October blacktail hunt that'd been delayed four days because of 70-mph winds. Had he seen bears?

"Oh yeah, we were eaten up," he said. "Three camp raids in seven nights. They ate our deer, ate their heads, ate their brains, ate their jaw bones; they especially seemed to love to eat their antlers. I woke up in a tent with three brown bears five feet away."

Gulp. He told me he hunted with a .25-06 (?!), and I imagined a hungry

TALL COUNTRY: This steep bluff overlook held a small buck early in the morning, and a big buck walked around the rock outcropping near dusk, appearing right where Knowles is standing in this photo hours after it was taken. Most of Kodiak is much brushier than this area, which is pounded by prevailing winds and rarely hunted because the weather limits boat access. Knowles' party only got to hunt it one day before the winds blew the harbor out.

brown picking his teeth with that thin barrel after eating him. "My friend had a bigger gun, though, a 7mm mag," he said. (A bigger gun? Really?) He'd killed a 71-inch moose with a 7mm the year prior, he said, and it had run 300 yards before dropping. On this trip, I was packing a Remington 700 XCR in .300 RUM, a black nitrite-coated stainless beauty shooting their 200-grain Swift A-Frame 3,000-plus-fps extended-range cartridges, topped with a Cabela's Alaskan Guide 3x9 scope. The gun is just over seven pounds, but with those loads it packs more energy than a .338, so it kills at both ends...an ideal deer gun for a place with 1,200-pound man-eating raccoons.

The bears are hardly hunted on tribal lands, "So we saw dozens of bears in seven days. All day, every day," he said. "They ate everything, even the skull plate; we just found

these little slivers of bone. If they come for your deer, they never stop."

A woman on the plane told of the heartbreak of bagging a huge buck after years on The Rock, of getting it down to the beach only to have The Man in the Brown Suit show up and pick it up like a Lab grabbing a newspaper and trot off with it. You could still see the disappointment in her eyes.

So...why bother? What is the obsession with these little deer? I was leaving Illinois, land of gagger whitetails, to hunt deer where a trophy is considered anything over 75 inches. This was like leaving Hawaii's North Shore to surf Lake Michigan. But in reality, hunting The Rock is everything that hunting used to be, the antithesis of walking through a field to hunt a woodlot whitetail in a place where even a kid couldn't get lost.

On Kodiak, you will see things you've never seen. Flying over the mountains toward Larsen Bay from Kodiak City, it was bigger country than I'd imagined. Giant slopes with

new snow that begged for a heli-drop by a ski video team. Two days later I would stand with Doug on a hillside and watch whales spout and roll off the point below, counting sea otters, when a golden eagle in full tuck dive at Mach speed ripped just over our heads within a few feet, startling us with the jet engine noise, as it tore into a flock of seagulls just below.

And the whole time, you have an eye on the bush, looking out for a giant bear, and another eye on the sky, watching for that treacherous weather to change. And, oh yeah, the deer.

On day one, Luke Hartle, the young tough guy from our party, shot a whopper 5x5 buck hot on a doe, just like that, a much bigger buck than he or I ever expected to see—16 to 18 inches wide, tall, tines sticking everywhere. The next day, Jay Cassell had a close chance at a good one, but his glasses fogged from rain. Soon after, he dropped a heavy 5x5 that ran out and started hooking a bush 50 yards from him, rubbing. The rut was on.

Turns out, though, Sitkas are no gimme. The rest of us had seen no bucks yet, and neither Luke nor Jay would see another good buck the rest of the trip. Despite the supposed 80 percent success rate on Kodiak, I talked to many guys in the airport who never saw a good deer. A whole group of bowhunters on another boat blanked for the entire week!

Luke and Jay had both hunted with Kodiak veteran Joe Arteburn of Cabela's, who is just a guy, not a guide...in theory. But they both described how he'd led them to their big bucks and muttered, "Shoot him." Arteburn either had the hot hand or was a great hunter, I didn't know yet. With glittery, mischievous eyes and a wry smile to off set the acerbic comments that puffed from the corner of his mouth that didn't have the pipe in it, he's a caricature of the seasoned woodsman, so I had a hunch. We all wanted to see if he could keep the streak going.

Hunters chase blacktails here many ways, landing in lakes by plane, tent camping or backpacking. The classic way to do it is a boat hunt out of Larsen Bay, gorging on halibut and crabs caught fresh, shooting ducks, the waves gently rocking you to sleep at night.

I'd anticipated an adventurous but easy hunt for little deer, but was wrong on every level. The hills are leg killers, for one thing. We quickly learned that the big bucks are rarely down low until a big snow, and getting dead deer out is brutal because there is no time for boning and packing meat 'cause that's a great way get a bear in your lap. It would prove one of the most physical hunts I'd endured as a lifelong elk maniac. And the deer are not small, but blocky-bodied brutes, 175 to 200 pounds, and to my delight, their antlers are plenty big to make your heart pound. The first three bucks we killed had great mass. One rack in the airport went 20 inches wide, and a photo from the Ninilchik charters site (ninilchik.

WE PUT AN EXCLAMATION POINT AT THE END OF THE VOYAGE BY JIGGING UP SIX HALIBUT.

com) showed a 130-plus monster a guy killed while it was standing on the beach with 13 other bucks, the kind of thing that can happen late in the season. Weather gets worse then, though, and if you wait too late their antlers start falling off. I saw only one good buck in six days. Heavy deer sign is everywhere, but the brush is so thick, there are few good areas to spot them.

Joe and I started day three in a bay with marvelous open vistas. It looked much like the Snake River country back home, much more open than the dense brush covering most of the island, but the area is only accessible in the rare event of nonprevailing winds. We spotted a smallish buck right off, and I wanted to take the 415-yard shot since I had two tags and enough gun, but the deer slipped away. Another memory: I started to walk off to relieve myself in some brush 20 yards away. "Take that with you," Joe said, nodding at the .300. "You never know where the bastards are gonna be." He was not talking about deer.

We hiked straight up, and while pinned to a steep hill, the same smallish buck popped out behind us on a bench where we'd eaten lunch. I decided if it's a three-point I was going to pop him since the trip was half over, I had another tag and I'd heard these were the best eating deer on earth. Then Joe whispered the f-word— "forky"—and I went limp, deflated.

We moved uphill and glassed amazing country. We saw deer, no good bucks. And after finding sunglasses and footprints, I was realizing that even though Kodiak is 90 percent wilderness, it's tough to access, so the boat captains tend to drop deer hunters in the same spots. These deer were definitely pressured.

The sun dropped, and we resigned to the day's failure, talking about tomorrow's hunt, working our way down. Breaking Joe's streak, and knowing I'd soon see another big buck hanging in camp, I was starting to feel like *that guy*. There was still a little light, so I picked a good spot, the lunch table bench where we'd seen the f-word buck, and told Joe we should watch it for 10 minutes, what the hell, and "besides, the thing wrong with today's hunt is you never smoked your pipe."

He agreed and pulled it out. Two minutes later I saw the buck, standing in deep golden grass on a steep shoulder below a rock outcropping where I'd stood myself five hours earlier. Even at 165 yards, he was a stunning creature, with white double chin patches and a

white chest against a dark chestnut coat, and the blackest black boss on his head. I could tell it was a buck, but not how big, making sure to peep through the scope instead of the binocs to avoid that rookie move, because the deer was alert. I asked Joe what he thought, but he was already covering his ears.

"Shoot him," he said with his entire face, mouthing the words. *"Shoot him."*

My heart raced, but the crosshairs were rock steady with the bipod.

The hike to the spot where the buck had stood took 20 minutes, it was so steep. I could smell the hot, musky scent of the deer, but could find no blood. As always, in that instant, I couldn't remember the shot clearly. He'd hunched and run back around the knob, faster than I could cycle the bolt. I could not believe my eyes—we were using monster bear loads... I had to think if I'd hit him he'd drop hard, if not back-flip. Yet the shot felt good.

Joe taught me something there: Do not quit watching after the shot, ever. He'd spotted alders shaking well

after the boom, and he found the buck 35 yards away, where he'd not only run from sight but blasted through a dense alder patch. With no blood, I'm not sure I'd have found the deer in time with darkness falling fast in the worst area in the world for predators. We found him jammed under a tree, a heavy 4x4, and I trembled with gratitude. Front shoulder smashed, opposing hindquarter smashed, everything between jelly, and this tough critter ran that far on two legs. Unreal. The cold reality: My cannon would drop no 1,200-pound angry bears instantly. I dressed the deer, handed Joe my pack and rifle while he watched for bear, and commenced the harshest deer drag of my life, a mile of hell down a steep muddy creek through log jams. The buck looked like it had suffered a bear mauling by the time we reached the bottom, and I had to pitch it over a short cliff to reach the beach. I hated to drag it, but to bone him out was to risk bad company. The thinking is, leave a gut pile and it may draw the bear away from you.

Bone-sore, exhausted and the pressure off, we took a field day the next morning, chasing fox and stunning Harlequin ducks on the beach all day, so the critter pile on the transom by sundown looked like a Turducken of fur and feathers, with five dead blacktail presiding and a few stiff cod I'd jigged up for crab bait bearing silent witness. Our hunt party camaraderie was something rare, with a duel of wit and practical jokes between our captain Rick and the young and mildly delinquent skipper of our sister boat, stealing each other's tender skiffs and such silliness.

The last day of the hunt, Cassell and I hit the timber and watched a small spike 250 yards away walk slowly toward us, hit our wind, spook, then calm down and finally pass within 15 feet of Jay, apparently deciding it was safe since we were not a bear. Just 30 yards uphill, we ran into snowshoe-sized tracks with four-inch claws, from a sow with cubs, and soon after more tracks from an enormous boar, all just a few hours old at most since a light snow fell that morning. We were covered in bears,

basically, and decided to only shoot a deer if it was a really big buck. Far away, we saw other hunters getting moved around by skiffs too early to quit, and without hearing shots. There could only be one reason for that, and I confirmed later that they'd run into an ornery sow and grown cubs, likely the same bears that had

I WOULD DO IT AGAIN JUST FOR THE CRAB FEAST.

terrorized me and Len on the first day. A big boar walked within 70 yards of our other party as well this last day. Fear Factor, right up to the end.

Yet this hunt is like nothing I've known. I love these beautiful deer and the wilderness they live in above the sea. The trip to The Rock is worth it for the whales and wildlife viewing, for the duck hunting, for the tour of the Alaskan Intercoastal and honestly,

I would do it again just for the crab feast. There's not too much to say about it, but I am still ecstatic about the pots we hauled full of giant tanner crabs. I've killed a lot of deer, but never gorged on crab like that. The Dungeness crabs I grew up on tasted like Krab-with-a-"k" by comparison. We put an exclamation point at the end of the voyage by jigging up six halibut just before we made port, enough for all to take home fresh slabs of Alaska's finest.

Throw in thrilling, sometimes terrifying spot-and-stalk hunting for beautiful big-bodied, delicious Sitka bucks and the Kodiak experience is an affordable, unguided, DIY hunt all the way. How else can a nonresident experience Alaska to this extent for $2,600?

And, it turns out, Kardiak Island is still plenty wild after all. It will be a long time before I no longer hear "the footsteps" when I first step into the bush. Ⓗ

PRONGHORN PANIC

J. GUTHRIE

"Time is of the essence." The phrase is overwrought and overused, but it certainly applies to humans and humans hunting. You hunt to escape the clock, only to live by it in the field. Seconds can cost us a shot. Minutes begin and end shooting light, and days define a season. Years start and stop our hunting altogether—time controls it all; it is inescapable.

Nowhere was time of the essence more than early this fall in New Mexico. I had an antelope tag and just two short days to get it done. That's right, the state gives hunters just two short days, two sunrises and two sunsets to spot, stalk and shoot a big, mature antelope. Two days to bring home a nice antelope, or two days to screw it all up. It was enough to make a man nervous, excitable, irritable—enough to make a man panic. How would time judge my performance during the great pronghorn panic of 2010?

WITH JUST TWO DAYS TO HUNT NEW MEXICO,
IT'S ENOUGH TO INDUCE PRONGHORN PANIC.

Most antelope hunts are leisurely affairs with four days or five—a veritable ice age compared with New Mexico's season—to pick a goat, stalk him, blow the stalk and try it again a dozen or two times until things finally go right. Not so in New Mexico. But at least I was in good hands. Kirk Kelso had been hunting the small ranch—if you can call 7,800 acres small—where we would be, and several others outside of Carrizozo, for 18 years and killed more than 100 bucks that would make the Boone & Crockett minimum. Kelso said some years, half the bucks tagged were over 82 B&C points. It is a stunning statistic, and I had a landowner's tag for this hallowed ground.

Kelso made his name hunting Coues deer in Arizona and Mexico, and I was fascinated reading the stories about his long-range shooting adventures some 20 years ago in this very magazine. He stumbled onto this ranch a short time after starting his outfitting business, and though he has since given up Coues hunting due to drastic changes south of the border, chasing antelope has proved too lucrative, too exciting to put down.

Though I have hunted antelope a half dozen other times with all sorts of tools, from muzzleloaders to handguns, my fear was making the mistake of shooting too small too early, or passing up too good and finding it too late to amend the mistake. Kelso, his 20X, gyro-stabilized Zeiss binoculars and vast experience would make it all OK.

As the opening-day sun rose on a chilly, high-desert plain, we waited for the pandemonium to begin, watching

the minutes tick by on a digital dashboard clock. Antelope started to appear out of the gloom. Bucks materialized on the horizon, across the fence on the neighbor's place and in the little flat to our front. Kelso checked them off like sixth-graders in homeroom. "Nice prongs, too short. Too young. Nice length, short on mass. Let him grow a few years." And just like that, we were off to another part of the ranch. Underlying every look, every word, was a sense of urgency. Even after 18 years, Kelso was feeling the pressure—you could rightly call it excitement—too.

Just a short 10- minute drive later, we slowed to a crawl as three different groups of antelope worked the flats and ridges around us from almost in rifle range to way the hell out there.

In the minute or so it took to look at one spot with the binos, then scan to another and look back, a small band of antelope appeared out of nowhere directly to our front. Flat this land is not, though driving down the interstate it looks as featureless and exciting as an airport runway. In this herd were two different bucks, a big one and a small one, and the former deserved a closer look. Three sets of high-end binoculars were locked to his every move, and the closer he came, the better he looked. And time, believe it or not, was on our side. Unspooked and unhurried, the groups had not a care in the world and did not appear to have that common antelope desire to be in the other end of the county.

That is one of the beauties of New Mexico's two-day season: It limits the hunting pressure. Antelope in most other states are necessarily bundles of frayed nerves

that scatter like tumbleweeds in a tornado at the first hint of a shot or even a pickup that quits powering through the dust and gravel and starts to coast. They can feel a funny look from hunters and head to the next county. Goats in New Mexico are mildly interested.

The buck and his does ambled over a ridge, out of sight and into a little bowl. We slipped out of the truck, chambered a round, bent over at the waist and scrambled up the ridge. A lone yucca sat on the skyline and provided enough cover that we all were able to peer around, over and under the spiny leaves without being spotted.

First I admired the buck through binos and quickly figured it was time to admire him through a riflescope. Any antelope hunter, novice or expert, could see that this was an exceptional buck in a land full of exceptional bucks. He was extremely heavy, and his cutters

The crosshairs rose to the right spot, thumping up and down with each heartbeat.

sat way above his ears. Kelso did not offer his thoughts on the buck, but he mentioned that the range was something on the order of 280 yards. He will only take you so far; pulling the trigger is up to you. The adrenaline kicked in, and the blood started to rush.

I hurriedly flipped out my shooting sticks and slapped the rifle down on top of them. I had memorized the drop chart of my .308 and knew the 150-grain Triple Shock would be around 11 inches low at that range. Mashing my face down on the stock and finding the sight picture to my liking, it was just seconds before the second stadia down on the reticle found its mark. I was on autopilot, or so I thought, and do not even remember knocking off the safety or running through a breath to empty my lungs for the shot.

That bullet should have been in the air just a touch over ⅓ of a second before striking the buck's shoulder,

but its flight time was infinitely longer. Kelso was kind enough to let me know that my shot went high and suggested I aim a little lower next time. The spinning wheels in my mind caught some traction, and as everything else in the entire world faded away except for a now-nervous and exceptional antelope buck making his way up the valley, time slowed to an absolute crawl.

The buck's hooves kicked up the slightest hint of dust with each step, and that was enough for a wind call. My drops had not changed, nor the aiming point. The second stadia found its mark—a touch of tawny hide showing below the inky black line would drop the bullet perfectly through the center of the buck's chest and smash both his lungs. I ran through a check of all that is holy to field marksmanship—my sticks were stuck firmly in the dirt, my elbows locked firmly into my knees, and my sight picture was perfect.

The buck stopped and looked back, anxious to find the source of the shot. Slower still the earth spun as I placed my finger on the trigger and let all the air out of my lungs. The crosshairs rose to the right spot, thumping up and down with each heartbeat. My finger tightened on the trigger and waited for the last bit of air to leave my body. With nothing left, I pulled the trigger rearward the way a fencepost shadow crawls across the sage.

A hammer fell, a firing pin snapped forward, a primer popped and powder burned. And in a millisecond the bullet was out of the barrel and recoil crashed my sight picture. Some fancy math tells me it took the bullet .35 second to reach the buck and the solid *thwack* of a good hit another full second to reach my ears. Ten seconds later, the buck piled up on grass. All the sights, sounds and time crashed the tunnel in which I was living,

and relief washed over me in waves as the shaking started.

After tagging, gutting and photographing the buck, I happened to look at the digital dash clock that started it all that morning and saw that it was just 9 a.m.

My hunt was marvelously successful, despite the panic-inducing limits of a two-day season. And the irony was not lost on me, as I rushed to the airport and worried about connection times and deadlines, that quiet had no doubt returned to the beautiful ranch outside of Carrizozo, as the antelope watched the clouds pass by and the sun set and rose, and still they marked no time. The generations of farmers and ranchers have and would come and go, the miners had come and gone, the conquistadors on their fine Spanish mounts must have been a curios sight, and the ghosts of Native American hunters still haunted the plains. But time, time that pushed and controlled all those who had passed through this high desert and hunted before me, still mattered not bit to the antelope. Ⓗ

HOG HEAVEN

DAVID HART

HOGS ARE EVERYWHERE.
GO HUNT THEM.
PLEASE.

Twenty years ago, wildlife managers were practically begging hunters to shoot more deer. The ubiquitous whitetail was being blamed for a spike in auto accidents, widespread crop damage, and an endless appetite for ornamental flowers and shrubs. These days, those same stories are being rewritten, only the word "deer" is being replaced with "hog." Feral pigs have become the 21st century's version of rats with hooves, vermin that destroy crops, devour critical wildlife habitat, and roto-till suburban lawns. But what's bad for ranchers, homeowners, and wildlife managers has been nothing but a boon for hunters. There's no question hogs are bad news. However, when life gives you lemons, why not pick up a .30-caliber lemon squeezer and go make a little lemonade?

SOUTH

Arguably, the best public feral hog opportunities can be found in the southeastern United States. And Florida ranks among the best state in the Southeast. Although the Florida Fish and Wildlife Conservation Commission doesn't know how many hogs are running loose in the Sunshine State, they are scattered across the entire state, with heavy concentrations in the central and northeastern region. FWCC spokesman Tony Young says the highest populations are west of Lake Okeechobee, in the state's western bend, and between the Kissimmee and lower St. Johns rivers. There are numerous public opportunities throughout the state, as well. Young says the Three Lakes, Green Swamp, Aucilla, Andrews and Dinner Island Ranch WMAs are tops in their regions.

Hunters do not need a license to hunt pigs on private land, but they do for public land. A few WMAs have bag limits and size restrictions, so consult the regulations before going afield.

Mississippi wildlife officials have no idea how many hogs they have either, but Mississippi Department of Wildlife, Fisheries and Parks Wildlife Coordinator Ricky Flynt says, "we have a bunch.

"They are all over the state, but they are concentrated in the Delta region and the extreme southeast and southwest corners of the state."

Public opportunities are not only abundant, they can be excellent, he adds. However, pig hunting opportunities on Department-owned wildlife management areas are restricted to open hunting seasons only. In other words, pigs cannot be hunted outside of deer, turkey, or other designated game seasons. They can, however, be hunted on private property year round, 24 hours a day, and without firearms restrictions.

Flynt says Pascagoula and Ward Bayou WMAs are exceptionally good; so are Caney Creek and Tallahala WMAs, which are located in east-central Mississippi. The Delta management areas of Lake George and Sunflower are also productive, says Flynt.

"They are a tremendous problem. We encourage hunters to shoot all they can," he says.

So does the South Carolina Department of Natural Resources. With an estimated 150,000 hogs and pigs in virtually every county in the state, DNR officials are hoping hunters will increase their harvest. They are, but not enough. Last season, hunters took about 36,000, up just two percent from the previous year.

"Most hogs are found in the Coastal Plain on private property, and getting permission by knocking on doors is just about impossible," says DNR biologist Charles Ruth. "We do have some WMAs that offer pretty good hog hunting, though. If you look at our website and see a special hog hunt outside of the normal hunting seasons, you can be sure that area has a whole lot of hogs."

Georgia also encourages hunters to shoot as many pigs as they can, and the state legislature even legalized hunting hogs over bait this year.

"Only on private land," says Georgia Department of Natural Resources senior wildlife biologist Don McGowan.

The agency doesn't have a handle on overall hog numbers, but McGowan says they are found throughout the state, and their numbers continue to increase, especially in the south and southeastern corner of the state where public opportunities are abundant. McGowan points to several WMAs along both the Altamaha and Oconee rivers, including Bullard Creek, Horse Creek, Riverbend, and Beaverdam WMAs.

He also says outstanding limited-entry hog hunts are available on several barrier island WMAs and national wildlife refuges.

"Ossabaw and Sapelo management areas have very good success rates," says McGowan. "So do Blackbeard Island, Cumberland Island, and Harris Neck national wildlife refuges. They are all drawing hunts."

WEST

The best bet for a western pig hunt lies within the borders of California. Wild pigs live in 56 of the state's 58 counties. The highest populations are centered around the San Joaquin Valley. Kern and Monterey counties accounted for 16.7% and 17.5 percent of the reported statewide harvest last year. Farther north, Mendocino, Shasta and Tehama counties were also top producers. Although public land is abundant in much of the state's feral pig range, the vast majority—94 percent—of the statewide harvest was taken on private land. Two military bases, Fort Hunter Liggett and Camp Roberts, accounted for a large percentage of the public land harvest, as well.

TEXAS IS TOPS

Contrary to popular belief, everything isn't leased in Texas, and with an estimated 2 to 2.6 million feral pigs, there's plenty of hunting opportunities. The Texas Parks and Wildlife Department has an abundant and productive public hunting system that consists of tens of thousands of acres of Department-owned land as well as national forest, state park, leased private property, Corps of Engineers land, and other cooperative properties. Some land is better than others for hog hunting, and TPWD Public Hunting Program Specialist Kelly Edmiston says some is downright fantastic.

"We have a draw hunt program where hunters can usually harvest feral hogs along with whatever other game animal they are hunting, but we also have nine specific draw hog hunts, and they can be extremely good," he says.

Hunters on White Oak Creek WMA, for example, enjoyed a 440 percent success rate. Dogs are allowed and so are off-road vehicles. Even still-hunt-only management areas can be exceptional, says Edmiston. He points to Mad Island WMA, where 38 hunters killed 47 hogs over six days. The draw hunts require an application and, if drawn, a fee of up to $80. However, the hunts typically run three days, and hunters are assigned a specific area. The hunts are popular, however. Hundreds can apply for some draw hunts, although just 67 hunters

applied for the 12 slots available at White Oak Creek.

"We also sell a $48 annual permit that's good for our walk-in public hunting areas. Some of those can be pretty good, but pigs are smart animals and respond accordingly to hunting pressure," says Edmiston.

What isn't public is indeed often leased, but with so many pigs and so many landowners struggling to keep hog numbers in check, hunts on private land can be cheap. Knocking on doors may be a long-shot, but individual ranchers may be willing to charge a nominal trespass fee, particularly outside of deer or turkey seasons. Hog hunting is open year round, and there are few restrictions. Hunters can chase swine 24 hours a day, and they can use a light and electronic calls.

MIDWEST

Despite a growing population and the accompanying problems, Missouri wildlife officials have had an about-face with their hogs. Instead of encouraging hunters to help knock pig numbers down, they have instead started discouraging hunters from hunting pigs. It's not because they want to boost hog numbers. Instead, says Missouri Department of Conservation Regional Supervisor Ken West, the agency is attempting to discourage hunters from importing more pigs.

"It's definitely a paradigm shift from what we were doing not too long ago. We certainly encourage people to shoot pigs on sight while they are deer hunting or participating in some other type of hunting, but we don't want people going out just for the purpose of hog hunting," says West. "I don't think we'll actually ban hog hunting, but we are still involved in some aerial eradication efforts as well as trapping efforts. Mostly, we just want people to stop transporting pigs from other states for the purpose of hunting them here."

With that said, "deer" hunters should look to the extreme southwest counties of Barry and Stone, which have abundant Forest Service land. According to the MDC web site, there is also a decent population of pigs on public land in Benton County, notably the Little Tebo Creek WMA and Corps of Engineers land. There is also a population in the southeastern Missouri counties of Iron, Reynolds, Madison and Washington.

Don't even think about hunting feral hogs in Kansas, which took an even harder line than Missouri. The Kansas Department of Wildlife and Parks banned hog hunting a few years ago to discourage the further importation of pigs. The agency is in the midst of its own eradication effort and wants no help from hunters.

Michigan is one of the most recent states to battle feral hogs, which were likely the result of illegal releases or escapees from fenced hunting preserves. Wherever they came from, the Michigan Department of Natural Resources wants them gone. Spokesman Mary Dettloff says anyone with a hunting license can shoot an unlimited number of pigs.

"We don't know how many there are, but we feel the population is growing," she says. "We are trying to establish them as an invasive species and the DNR wants to regulate enclosed facilities. Basically, we want them eradicated from the state."

At least 261 feral hogs have been taken in 51 counties, including several in the Upper Peninsula, since 2002, although no particular county stands out.

Ohio is also battling an increase in hogs. There are only 1,000 or so, but they are spread out, with pockets of pigs in at least 28 counties. The heaviest concentration is in the southeast, but pigs are also thriving in western Ohio. There is no limit and no closed season, but public opportunities are somewhat limited.

There doesn't seem be a limit to where feral hogs can live, either. They are also found in Tennessee, Indiana, New York, North Carolina, Oklahoma, and at least two dozen other states, even Wisconsin. While wildlife managers in the few states that don't have hogs yet don't want them, hunters will certainly do their share to help keep them in check if they show up. Ⓗ

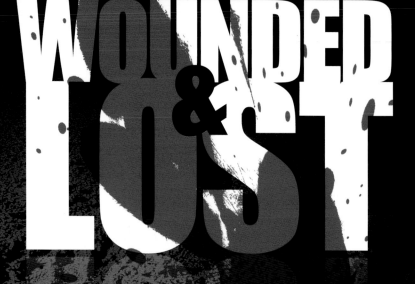

WOUNDED & LOST

CAN WE TALK ABOUT THIS?

have a friend who, unfortunately, is a rare bird in our world. He's a magazine editor, but he's also a serious hunter, a great shot, a fine writer and a good photographer. From what I can see, he possesses great people skills as well as a clear vision for our sport and the media that support it. He's a lot younger than I am, but I see a younger me in him. I hope he sticks around, because I think he has a very bright future—and our sport needs guys like him. No, it isn't Mike Schoby, although all of these things apply to our current editor. And, no, he isn't on staff on this magazine, so quit speculating.

Anyway, this guy with all the skills and talents—he's in pretty good shape, too—went on a brown bear hunt in Alaska this past year. The hunting gods—or gremlins—dealt him a shot at a fine bear that he was properly armed for and capable of handling. Except, somehow, things went terribly wrong. The bear was wounded, and the trail quickly evaporated. Despite days of effort, no further trace was seen. The bear was lost.

My friend is a tough guy, but he was crushed. Obviously, this was a very important hunt; at this stage in his career, a dream come true . . . had turned into a nightmare. He's having trouble getting past it, admitting to lack of confidence and, since then, hesitation that has cost him new opportunities. This is a subject we simply don't talk about. Wounding and losing an animal is one of the serious downsides to hunting. It's a horrible thing for the animal, an obvious waste of a resource, and, for the hunter, it should be and usually is a catastrophic emotional event. But since we don't talk about it, there isn't much help out there in trying to deal with it. Can we talk about it?

CRAIG BODDINGTON

We all have "comfort zones" for our field shooting; familiar circumstances tend to reduce the risk, while unfamiliar areas and animals—and stressful shooting situations—greatly increase the risk of a bad shot.

PART OF THE DEAL

In recent years a lot of the social taboos I grew up with have come out of the closet, so to speak. Regardless of your opinion on the subject, gay-lesbian issues are in the news every day. Men never even whispered about what we will delicately call "ED," but today we can't watch a TV show without seeing a Viagra or Cialis ad (snicker, snicker, er, honey, where are those pills?). Surely we can talk about shots that go wrong— because sometimes, with the very best of intentions, they do. Wounding a fine animal and not recovering it is a serious thing. It should never be taken lightly. If you don't become physically ill when it happens, there's something wrong with you . . . and if you don't take every measure possible to recover the animal, then you don't deserve the title "hunter."

Unfortunately, it does happen. For most of us it is (and should be!) a very rare event. Rare enough that there are many hunters reading these lines to whom it has never happened . . . yet. More about that later. There are innumerable reasons why it happens. Usually it happens because the shot didn't go where it was supposed to go. This can be a result of nerves, a hurried shot from an unsteady position, failure to properly visualize the animal's presentation, an animal that is moving—or moves just as the shot is fired. One could argue that all of these things are the hunter's fault in taking a shot that wasn't certain. OK, you bet . . . it is the hunter's fault, which is the first thing we must accept. Might as well accept that we're all human, we all get excited and we all make mistakes. Most of the time we get away with it, either

with a clean miss or a bullet intended for the boiler room hits the neck— instead of the other end. But sometimes we don't get away with it. More rarely, a wounded animal can result from a cartridge inadequate for the game, or a bullet that didn't perform, or a scope that mysteriously goes out. It seems part of our society today to always shift blame elsewhere. Equipment issues can lead to disasters—but we choose our equipment and have the responsibility to make sure it's adequate for the job as well as working properly, so I still think the person who pulls the trigger or releases the arrow must accept full responsibility for a lost animal.

NOT THE WORST

I don't want to make light of such an event. It is a personal crisis, but it happens, and you must get past it. On the other hand, I am not a member of PETA and I don't subscribe to their "a dog is a rat is a pig is a boy" mantra. There are worse things that can happen on a hunting trip. As is well-known, my daughter was involved in a shooting accident on a hunt a couple of years ago. A doctor friend of mine was a teenager when his best friend shot him in a dumb accident. He's my age and has had a great career—but he's never walked properly. He's still an avid hunter, and his friend is still his friend. My daughter is still getting over it, but she's still hunting. Our sport is not particularly dangerous when compared to things like skydiving, virtually all forms of racing and almost anything to do with horses, but stuff happens. I had a serious health incident on safari last year. I've seen guys break bones and have other traumatic injuries, and every year a few hunters are going to die while pursuing their passion. So let's get real about this. Wounding and losing a fine animal is a terrible thing. Chances are, unfortunately, the animal won't get over it. The hunter can, and must … or must quit. This last seems a silly solution, because hunting is part of who we are, not just part of what we do. And, once in a while, things will go wrong.

GLASS HOUSES

In my 50 years of hunting and 40 years of writing about it, I have never specifically addressed this subject, but I have touched around the edges. I know that some of you out there—to whom it has never happened (yet!)—are getting out pen and paper. Please

be careful. We are all living in glass houses, so starting a rock-throwing event may not be the wisest course. Believe me, it can happen . . . and it can happen to you. Whether it ever will depends somewhat on your luck, your experience and how you hunt.

Mind you, it can happen to anybody—at any time. But if you do most of your hunting very deliberately, perhaps from familiar stands in friendly territory, properly organized with a good rest and known distances all around, then your risk is reduced. (But it can still happen.) If you hunt a lot on foot, especially in rough country or thick cover where exertion and fleeting opportunities play a larger role, then your exposure is increased. Realistically, if you hunt with bow, blackpowder, handgun, iron sights or even slug guns, your risk goes up. In my view that doesn't make it all right; it just means the odds are higher.

Yes, it has happened to me. It's happened to me more than once, and although I don't think my buddy knew this when he suggested this story, it happened to me on a really great bear. I was on a knoll in Southeast Alaska, and a beautiful brown bear stepped out of the brush about a hundred yards below me. I rested over the packframe and took what I thought to be a very good shot, and the bear rolled into the brush, gone. I should have had time to fire again, but it was a classic sin of admiring the shot. We had good blood on both sides of the trail, complete penetration and it looked good. It looked less good after the bear swam a beaver pond . . . and after the third such pond there was no trail at all. We searched for the rest of the hunt, but no further sign was

found. Was I sick? Oh, yeah. I guess I flubbed the shot a bit forward, because that bear was seen again the following season, hale and hearty—but even that doesn't make me feel much better. I relive that shot over and over . . . especially my failure to fire again!

As a writer I have long tired of colleagues who shoot better with their computers than with their hunting arms. I've been in this business long enough that I've seen most of them shoot! So I have consciously gone the other way, often emphasizing my (many) mistakes, and downplaying the good shots. This has resulted in the occasional letter suggesting that if I really shoot that badly I shouldn't be in the field. That's from The Law of Unintended Consequences (we'll discuss Murphy's Law next). Realistically, I shoot pretty well and have the credentials in multiple disciplines to prove it. Also realistically, at nearly 60 I'm not as limber as I once was, nor do I have the eyes and reflexes I had 40 years ago. Experience does mitigate this somewhat; I do miss shots, and I have wounded and lost game—but I'm not yet seeing a dramatic increase in either. As you get out your pen and paper, let me just say that over the course of 50 years, I can count my wounded and lost animals with the fingers of both hands. I can recall each incident with painful clarity, and I hope I have learned something from each—but I've been actively hunting for a long time, and these represent something less than one percent of the game I've taken.

So, as you get ready to write, keep in mind that one's hunting career isn't a sprint; it's an ultra-marathon, and

IF YOU DON'T BECOME PHYSICALLY ILL WHEN IT HAPPENS, THERE'S SOMETHING WRONG WITH YOU...

it isn't over 'til it's over. I call to mind the old-time gunwriter Ned Crossman, who wrote, albeit on choosing rifles and cartridges, "After all, the digest of a hundred men—picked men, not chaps who once killed a buck in the Adirondacks and know all about game rifles—is the best way to reach an intelligent decision." If it hasn't happened to you, then you are fortunate. But pride goeth before a fall, and Mr. Murphy lies in wait. It can happen, and if you hunt enough it probably will. Do all you can to avoid it, but be mentally prepared, and understand you aren't the first, last or only hunter this has happened to.

MURPHY'S LAW

As I alluded to earlier, some situations are riskier than others. We all have different comfort zones, whether it's a deer stand behind the house or shooting sticks in African thornbush. When you get out of your comfort zone and must deal with unfamiliar country and unknown animals, the risks go up. Larger animals may be easier to hit, but larger animals are often much harder to kill. Bears are especially tough, and there's something about the fur and dark,

blocky body that seems to make shot placement more difficult than it ought to be. Although I've flubbed brain shots on elephants, I can honestly say that I've never had to track an elephant I've shot and have certainly never lost one—but although we never talk about such things, a lot of elephants are lost because hunters insist on the classic brain shot.

Buffalo are even worse. In recent years, spending a lot of time in the Zambezi Valley, it seems to me that the wounded-and-lost rate on buffalo approaches a very high and totally unacceptable 10 percent. I've lost buffalo, but nothing like that percentage, so I'm probably way ahead of the curve. Again, it's a black animal, seeming to confound shot placement ... and it's also very strong. Some buffalo will circle and lie in wait, but in my experience the most likely thing to happen when a buffalo is hit poorly is that he is simply never seen again.

There are special circumstances. Although shots on sheep can be very difficult, especially in the big, open mountains of Asia, sheep tend to be fairly soft and are usually recovered. Goats are much tougher and when hit poorly often take themselves into

dangerous stuff where recovery becomes suicidal. One of the worst situations I know of is the mountain nyala in Ethiopia. There aren't many, and they're difficult to find, so there is much pressure on the shot. But they're also tough, more like a giant bushbuck than a kudu, and the high heather they live in is so thick as to be almost impenetrable. I know relatively few people who have hunted this legendary beast—but among them I can count at least six hunters who have wounded and lost their mountain nyala, a very high number. When I took my second (and last) mountain nyala, I was on sticks looking out over high heather, and all I could see was the head and neck of a fine bull. The distance wasn't great and the rifle was superbly accurate. I shot him right behind the ear, and he dropped. But in retrospect, what in the world was I thinking? The best way to avoid wounded and lost animals is to pass on risky shots. But most of us, me included, lack total restraint. If you pull off a tough shot, you're a hero, but Mr. Murphy is always right beside you. If you don't pull it off, you've joined a fairly large and not-so-exclusive club.

GET BACK ON THE HORSE

A wounded animal can haunt you for months, if not for years. It depends a lot on how often you're able to get into the field, and thus how much time you must brood and mope before your next outing. It is not a good thing to simply forget about it. The best thing you can do is try to learn from your mistakes ... and, more importantly, try not to repeat them. Stuff happens,

Bigger animals are easier to hit—but not necessarily in the right places. An unfortunate number of elephants are wounded and lost, often due to the insistence on the classic brain shot and lack of quick follow-up.

and you aren't alone. It's best to get back on the horse as quickly as you can. Accept a loss as a most unfortunate part of the sport and go forward armed with new knowledge and perhaps a little extra humility. Hopefully it will never happen again . . . but if you hunt enough, there is a law of averages out there.

AFRICA RULES

One thing that's a bit different here in North America than in most of the rest of the world is that, elsewhere, and especially in Africa, one drop of blood counts for the license. In the case of the mountain nyala, the current license is $15,000, payable up front, and there is no reclama. That's several times more than when I last hunted them in 2000, but a deal like that should tend to make one very, very careful about taking the shot! A lost nyala, or a lost buffalo or elephant, any of the big ticket items, is obviously a financial as well as an emotional disaster, but I tend to like the concept that a wounded animal counts on the license.

Over here, all too often I fear we take more of a cavalier approach, look a little bit (or a lot), and then continue the hunt. That is generally within the limits of the law, but I think that attitude takes the situation too lightly. Sometimes, in many places, a second animal of the same species is legally available. If so, once the search is truly exhausted, I think it's just fine to continue—but my general feeling where there's just one tag is that a wounded animal fills that tag. The hunt should be concluded, the remainder spent looking for that animal. I note that more and more outfitters are following this rule, but of course, when we hunt alone, as we often do in our home territories, this and all other ethical nuances are totally up to us. Fortunately, this hasn't happened to me very often . . . and I certainly hope it never happens again. Touch wood, because Mr. Murphy is right there. Ⓑ

A Blond Moment

MANITOBA OFFERS MANY THINGS FOR BEAR HUNTERS... COLOR IS JUST ONE OF THEM.

WORDS & IMAGES by
MIKE SCHOBY

The Steller's jay sitting in the small pine tree quit squawking and looked nervously around. Something had bothered it. It swiveled its head side to side, trying to confirm its sixth sense. Whether the fear was real or imagined, the bird flushed, sailing through the trees and out of sight. My senses were on edge, ears straining to hear the slightest sound, eyes searching behind every piece of brush and limb for a patch of black. Nothing. Then I heard it, the slightest swish. The white noise sounded like nothing in particular, but to a bear hunter it sounded like everything. I couldn't see him, but I knew a bear had just arrived.

I sat statue-still, swiveling just my eyes, not risking to move my head under the camo facemask. A mosquito buzzed around my ear and settled on the skin between my lobe and neck. I felt him take a tentative step then pause, getting ready to feed. As the proboscis met skin, pure instinct fought with reason as I decided to not swat him. Another swish of hair against a wet branch floated through the air. This time I was able to mark the sound 30 yards away, somewhere off to my right. I slowly turned my head, eyes reaching first, chin following, as slow as a sundial. I stopped when I saw a patch of black that didn't look quite right.

The black spot

first looked like shadow, then the shadow shifted position. It was a bear and a cautious one at that. He stood downwind of the bait, partially hidden by brush, testing the wind. His head lifted and turned as his nostrils flared in and out, taking in the delicious smells of doughnuts, grease and molasses, but at the same time searching for the repugnant smell of man. Satisfied no one was immediately present, the bear took one tentative step out of the bush. Coal black with a white chevron on his chest. My heart sank when I saw the bear was mid-sized—a shooter in other parts of the world, but not in Manitoba. I looked at the bear again, trying to shrink his ears and grow his belly. He was almost there, but one lesson I have learned about bears is if you have to convince yourself he is big, he isn't. You never look twice at a true shooter, you just raise the rifle.

He came in, taking over the bait pile, settling in, completely relaxed, feeding until darkness obscured the scene. Even when I could no longer see him, I could occasionally hear the chain tethering the barrel to the tree rattle like a ghost walking a hallway in the night. After 15 minutes crept by without a sound, I snapped on my headlamp to scan the ground. No beady eyes reflected back. Silently packing my gear into my pack, I felt for the top rung on the ladder with my boot. I lowered myself to the ground and trudged through the dark swamp, following the flashlight's beam to the two-track road 20 minutes away. I could have had Rick or Colleen Liske from Agassiz-Waterhen River Lodge (agassizoutfitters.com) come in and pick me up with a four-wheeler, but the extra noise and smell don't help your chances of tagging a bruin.

Rick was waiting with his pickup on the road. "See anything?"

"Just one bear. All black, medium sized . . . not a shooter."

"Another night. The hunt is still early."

"Anybody else see anything?"

"Yeah, Jeff had a blond bear on his stand. It came out early around five and sat there most of the evening."

"Pure blond, not cinnamon? That's cool. How much did it weigh"

"I would guess 175 pounds."

"Guess?'

"Yeah. He let it walk"

"You got to be kidding me—he didn't shoot it?"

"Nope, he's looking for a huge bear."

"OK, I get that, but it's a blond bear? Does he know how rare that is?"

"He knows."

When we got back to the lodge, Jeff showed me the video. It was a gorgeous bear. He was right, it wasn't huge, but it was beautiful.

"Are you having second thoughts?" I asked.

LUCKILY, WHEN A BEAR BLEEDS THIS MUCH, THE TRAIL WON'T BE LONG OR HARD TO FOLLOW.

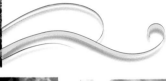

"Yeah, I probably should have shot him, but I really want a massive bear. But if he comes back in tomorrow, I think I will take him."

Deep down I knew that bear would never come back in, but I wished him well as we all turned in.

The following day, I learned why my hunting partner Bob Kaleta of Zeiss returns to this lodge every year . . . the bear hunting is out of this world. Not only are there lots of color phase bears, there are some massive bears as well. While my stand was cold, Bob's was red-hot, and he put the hurt on a bruiser of a boar right at dark. His .338 Win. Mag. only

barked once, but once was enough to anchor the 7-foot, all-black bruin. He and Rick could barely roll the ungutted boar onto the low-slung trailer towed behind the four-wheeler. His coat was thick and lush with a massive white band across the chest.

I knew the answer when I asked, "Are you going to full body mount him?" Bob is a bear freak who loves big boars, and his trophy room looks like a Cabela's showroom. His ear-to-ear grin confirmed my suspicions, and he said, "I don't know how I can't, but I have no idea how I am going to explain this to the wife." We skinned the brute that night, listening to the

loons on the river behind the skinning shed, sipping Molsons and retelling the day's hunt. A perfect cap to a perfect day.

Later on that night, at our ritualistic midnight dinner, Jeff finally staggered in from the field.

"Did you get one?" I asked.

"'Blondie' came back."

"And . . . ?"

"I passed him again."

I couldn't believe it, but then, that is bear hunting—everyone has their own idea of what constitutes a marvelous bear. Some hunters are driven by color, some covet size, others fancy skulls— to each his own. I have been fortunate enough to shoot some exceptionally large-skulled bears, but never much color, so the blond was really tripping my trigger.

"Man, that bear is lucky. If he was hitting my bait, I couldn't pass him."

"Do you want to sit there tomorrow? I have decided I am not going to shoot him, and he is all that is coming into that bait. I want to move anyway."

"DO I WANT TO SHOOT HIM? Does a bear . . . never mind. Yes, I will gladly take you up on the offer."

The next afternoon about 3 p.m., Colleen drove me to the stand. It was the closest stand to the lodge, perhaps five miles away, and Blondie had been coming in around 5 p.m. for the past two days.

"I'll drive back over around 8 o'clock," she said. "I won't come into the stand but will wait on the main road. If you shoot Blondie early, walk out to the main road, and I'll pick you up. If you don't get a shot, stay in the stand, I'll come get you around 11 p.m."

By the time I got into my stand it was 3:30. Summer was starting to

break free of spring, and the sun bea down overhead, making the day unseasonably warm. Unpacking my bag, I settled in for a prolonged evening. Even though the bear came in early for Jeff, I knew that probably wasn't in the cards. With my luck, Blondie would come at last light—if he made an appearance at all.

I had just settled in and decided to get comfortable. Leaning my rifle against the large stand's wood railing, I adjusted my spare jacket behind my head and was planning on taking a 30-minute catnap. I was beat tired from the late nights, the large lunch and the hot sun. I had just closed my eyes when I got a premonition that sleeping in the stand was not the best way to get a bear. I opened one eye and noticed Blondie had arrived. Unaware I was even there, Blondie was elbow deep in bait and going for more. Jeff was right, he wasn't massive, but he was big enough and absolutely gorgeous—blond down the back, brown head and cinnamon legs. I could no more pass him than I could pass dessert at Thanksgiving.

I slowly reached down and grabbed my Wild West CoPilot .45-70 and lifted it above the railing. The bear quit feeding and sat up. I centered the glowing red dot of the Zeiss Compact Point behind his shoulder and squeezed the trigger. The 350-grain Buffalo Bore bullet dropped the bear on the spot. I did not cycle the gun but waited to see if he got up. He finally twitched a paw then jumped to his feet. Remaining perfectly silent after the shot paid dividends as he ran directly toward my stand unaware of where the shot had come from. I threw the lever and put another bullet into the running bear, which bowled him head over tail. Regaining his feet he turned and entered the brush where I put a third and final shot in him. He died less than 10 yards from the bait pile.

I climbed down from the stand and approached the beautiful bear. Running my fingers through his long, luxurious hair, I knew I had just shot a bear of a lifetime.

With at least six hours and thousands of mosquito bites until a four-wheeler arrived, I weighed my options. No cell service, no radios, the only option I had was my two feet. If I walked to the main road, I was within five miles of camp—less than two hours. With any luck, I might even be able to thumb a ride once I hit the main highway. Shouldering my pack and carrying the lever gun, I felt like John Wayne walking into the sunset. I hit the main road within a half an hour and stuck out a thumb at an approaching car. They slowed . . . just enough to confirm that, yes, I was in full camo and carrying a lever-action rifle before speeding up, leaving me in a cloud of exhaust fumes and burning rubber smoke.

I kept walking and stuck out my thumb to every passing car only to get a repeat performance of the first. I covered four of the five miles and had given up any hope of hitching a ride when I heard a large vehicle approaching from behind. I didn't even bother to look around or stick out a thumb. Then I heard the cadence of the engine change and the rumble of gears being downshifted. Looking over my shoulder, I saw a semitruck slowing down behind me. "What kind of lunatic would pick up a gun-toting stranger?" I thought to myself. As the truck got closer I realized it wasn't a semitruck at all but a septic pump truck. Stopping next to me the driver rolled down his window. "I figure you are going to Waterhen lodge, want a

lift?" he asked. With only a mile to go I could walk to the lodge in another 15 minutes. Instead, I grabbed the door handle and climbed aboard. I mean, how often do you get to fulfill two Bucket List accomplishments in one day? Ahh, killing a blond bear and arriving back to the lodge in a shit truck—it doesn't get much better than that. Ⓗ

20

THE TWENTY-YEAR BULL

Colorado's Unit 2 is tough to draw but worth the wait.

WORDS & IMAGES by
DAVID HART

A DEEP DRAW and a fence marking the line between public and private land divided us, but the bull was hot, bugling every few minutes. Despite the obstacles, we figured we had nothing to lose, so my cousin and I backed into a thicket of juniper trees 30 yards from the edge of the draw and settled in. Shannon pulled a bugle from his pack and sent a warbling scream through the still Colorado morning. The bull answered immediately.

The sound of rocks tumbling down the hill sent a rush of adrenaline through my body. He was coming and he was coming fast. In less than a minute, I spotted antlers over the lip of the draw as the elk stopped to look for the challenger. When he couldn't find one, he climbed to the top, took a few more steps, and crossed the sagging fence. He stood facing us at just 18 yards.

I knew right away this bull, a wide 5x5 with average mass and tines, wasn't what we came for, so I lifted my head above the scope for one last look as he turned and disappeared back down the hill to safety. Anywhere else he would have been a good one, but not here, not in an area that is arguably the best public elk area in the country. Besides, the bull walked into range within the first five minutes on the first day of the hunt, and with four other bulls bugling in the distance, we knew other opportunities would come. As soon as we settled our nerves and exchanged grins, my cousin and I took off after another bull not 200 yards away. This one sounded big, his deep, bellowing bugles ending in an unmistakable roar.

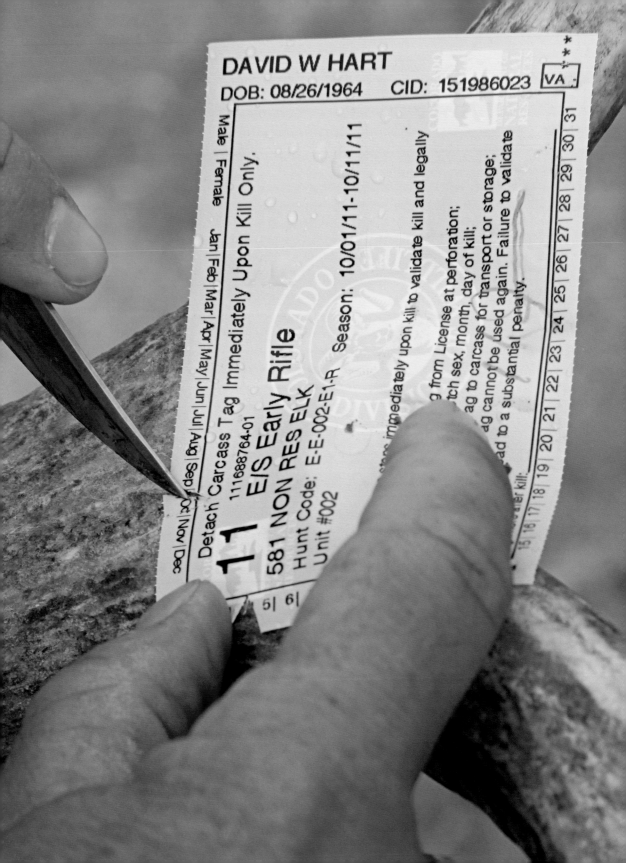

A TWENTY-YEAR QUEST

TWENTY YEARS AGO, my cousin and lifelong hunting partner, Shannon Sheffert, and I started applying for preference points with our eyes on Colorado's northwestern corner. It's here that several game management units, including Unit 2, are placed under lock and key, through a limited number of tags, in an effort to provide a high-quality hunting opportunity. Fourteen years into our application efforts, we were certain our time was close. But somewhere during our wait, the Colorado Division of Wildlife restructured the tag allotments, essentially moving the end zone and making it harder for nonresidents to draw. We considered using our points for an easier draw-only unit, but after waiting this long, we decided to stick it out. It would just be a matter of patience. Still, when I opened the envelope from the DOW last summer I fully expected another refund check. I instead pulled out a blue piece of paper marked "License, Unit #002, NON RES ELK." I looked at it and then looked again, stunned that I was holding not another check, but a tag that I had waited 20 years to draw.

I flew into Denver three days before opening day and was met by my cousin who pulled a camper from his home in Stillwater, Oklahoma. In anticipation of this day, Shannon had drawn cow elk tags for Unit 2 on three different occasions, mostly as an excuse to learn the country for our future bull hunt. It would prove instrumental to our success.

Five hours later, with just 15 minutes of daylight left, we parked the truck on the side of a road where Shannon had found bulls on earlier hunts and took off in opposite directions. I was immediately greeted by bugles just a few hundred yards away and at least two more in the distance. I crept toward the coarse screams and spotted a 5x5, not a giant but a good bull nonetheless and a great start to our scouting efforts.

Typical of elk country anywhere, Unit 2 is a vast area, 1,200 square miles, with pockets of elk and great expanses void of elk. Although we found sign just about everywhere we looked in two hard days of scouting, some areas were clearly better than others. But the comparisons ended there. Instead of towering lodgepoles, deep, dark timber and aspen parks, Unit 2 is high desert and is dotted with junipers, most no taller than a ceiling and spread far enough apart that it's not unusual to see several hundred yards or even several miles in the rolling hills and mountains. There are some Ponderosa pines on the highest points and vast open grass flats, but mostly, the country consists of junipers and sagebrush that span for miles.

COVERED IN ELK, SURROUNDED BY BUGLES

THOSE TREES, however sparse, can be just as daunting as the deep timber found in most elk country. We closed within a hundred yards of the second bull and tracked his movement by the distinct bugles that ended in a coarse bellow, certain he would show himself through one of the openings we were watching. I sat with my rifle propped up on a pair of shooting sticks, trembling in anticipation. But unlike the first bull that came on a string, this bull wanted nothing to do with the bugles and cow calls we threw at him. We followed but never caught up to him as he headed for private land. In fact, that's how much of the hunt played out. My cousin and I closed in on numerous bulls each day, only to have them move faster than we were moving. It was as if we were chasing ghosts. Should we have been

more aggressive? It was a question we debated each time we were beaten. We did catch up to several throughout the hunt, including seven that strolled past us in a parade of antlers and bugles, all within 200 yards, as darkness fell on the third evening.

In fact, we saw more bulls than cows in four days of hard hunting, an unusual ratio in most of the state, where cows can outnumber antlered bulls by five or more to one. Only one was a spike. Some were respectable 5x5s, and a couple were good 6x6s. But "good" in the rest of elk country is only marginal in Unit 2, where antlers scoring 300 inches are hardly worth a second look. We watched one big 5x6 strut in and out of the junipers later on the first day, offering occasional glimpses of his high, heavy crown, but he stayed across the fence that separated public and private ground. Five yards closer and I would have pulled the trigger. Soon after, another big bull, a 6x6, trailed a cow across a canyon, and I had my rifle up and the safety off. This one, however, never offered a good shot. Although it was impossible to count, we figured we heard at least 6,000 bugles, maybe even more, the first day alone. The screams started at first light and didn't stop as we headed back to the truck at dark.

Despite the limited number of bull tags allotted for this unit—just 51 rifle tags are handed out for the early season— and the overwhelming vastness of the area, it's not out of the question to bump into other hunters. The early rifle season opens October 1 while the rut is still on, so a bugling bull just might draw another hunter. As my cousin and I were putting a stalk on the third (or was it the fourth?) rut-crazed bull early on the first day, we bumped into a hunter and his two companions who were moving on the same elk. We would see their boot prints the rest of our hunt, but we never ran into them again. Their presence and ours, however, pushed the elk onto private property and made things tougher as the hunt progressed.

After three days of chasing bulls and not getting close to one of the giants that make this region one of the most coveted in the country, I was beginning to have doubts. Success rates for the early rifle season in Unit 2 averaged 74 percent over the last five years, but that means one out of four hunters fails to connect on a bull. Was I going to be one of them? I could have easily pulled the trigger on a number of bulls, but I didn't wait 20 years for a marginal 6x6. That night, my cousin and I mulled our options. We had backup areas, but none had as much sign as the area we had been hunting, so Shannon and I decided to stick with the area we knew was full of bulls. With the rut still going strong, we were certain there had to be a dominant bull that would cross onto the public land in his search for cows.

The fourth morning again found us on the edge of the ranch that held so many bulls, many still bugling beyond our reach. One, however, was clearly on public land, so we moved quickly to take a look, but like so many others, this one was moving away fast, staying out of sight as we hustled to catch up. He bugled again, this time across a sage flat but still out of sight. We finally spotted a cow and spike trotting through the junipers across the clearing, followed by a tall, wide 6x6 that stepped into an opening as he followed the cow. My cousin urged me to shoot, but I was already bracing my rifle over my shooting sticks. There was no question this was a good one. I flicked off the safety, centered the crosshairs on the bull's chest, and squeezed the trigger as it stepped through the narrow opening between two junipers.

I missed. A rush of emotions washed through me. Twenty years and I blew the best opportunity on the biggest bull of the hunt. How could I miss an elk at 200 yards? But just as quickly as things went downhill, fate gave me another opportunity. The bull reappeared in the opening, looking back as if he was wondering what just happened. I again centered the crosshairs on the bull's chest as he was quartering toward me and squeezed the trigger.

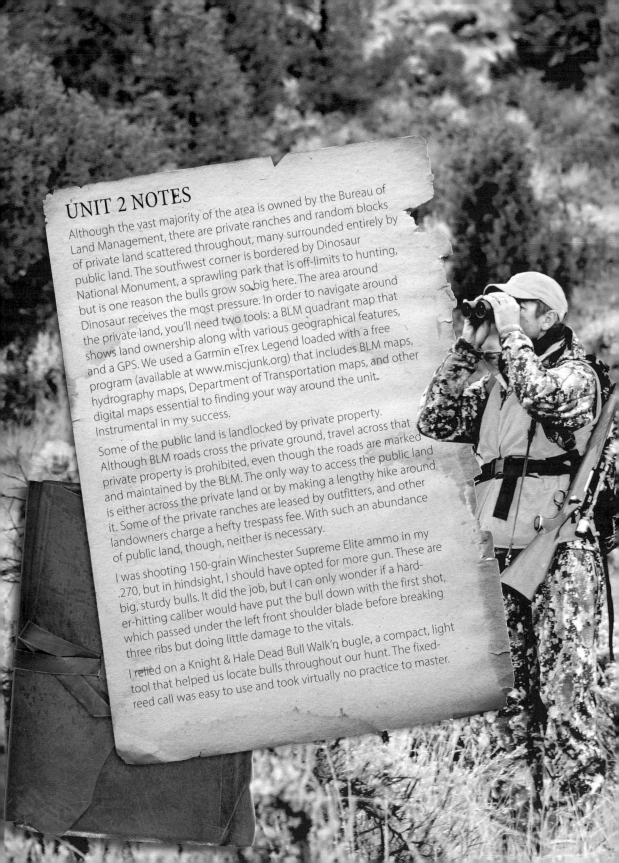

UNIT 2 NOTES

Although the vast majority of the area is owned by the Bureau of Land Management, there are private ranches and random blocks of private land scattered throughout, many surrounded entirely by public land. The southwest corner is bordered by Dinosaur National Monument, a sprawling park that is off-limits to hunting, but is one reason the bulls grow so big here. The area around Dinosaur receives the most pressure. In order to navigate around the private land, you'll need two tools: a BLM quadrant map that shows land ownership along with various geographical features, and a GPS. We used a Garmin eTrex Legend loaded with a free program (available at www.miscjunk.org) that includes BLM maps, hydrography maps, Department of Transportation maps, and other digital maps essential to finding your way around the unit. Instrumental in my success.

Some of the public land is landlocked by private property. Although BLM roads cross the private ground, travel across that private property is prohibited, even though the roads are marked and maintained by the BLM. The only way to access the public land is either across the private land or by making a lengthy hike around it. Some of the private ranches are leased by outfitters, and other landowners charge a hefty trespass fee. With such an abundance of public land, though, neither is necessary.

I was shooting 150-grain Winchester Supreme Elite ammo in my .270, but in hindsight, I should have opted for more gun. These are big, sturdy bulls. It did the job, but I can only wonder if a hard-er-hitting caliber would have put the bull down with the first shot, which passed under the left front shoulder blade before breaking three ribs but doing little damage to the vitals.

I relied on a Knight & Hale Dead Bull Walk'n bugle, a compact, light tool that helped us locate bulls throughout our hunt. The fixed-reed call was easy to use and took virtually no practice to master.

Northwest Colorado is steeped in history. The land is high desert, making it a tough place to eke out a living for current and former residents alike.

This time, we heard the thump of bullet hitting home. The elk turned again and slipped behind a tree, his antlers towering above the short juniper. The crown swayed back and forth, teetering as if the bull was about to fall over dead. Instead, it turned and disappeared into the thick junipers. I was again consumed by a sickening feeling. Was it down or were we destined to chase a crippled elk the rest of the afternoon? I was ready to rush over and start searching, but my cousin held me back, insisting we wait 15 minutes. As we got up after what seemed like an hour, I spotted the bull staggering away from us through a screen of limbs, clearly hurt but walking out of sight again. We circled downwind, found blood, and followed it to the edge of a rim. The bull lay in a copse of junipers just 20 yards away, looking back at me. He stood, took three steps, and turned broadside, standing still as if he knew the hunt was over. I threw my rifle up, pulled the trigger, and put an end to a 20-year hunt. ⓗ

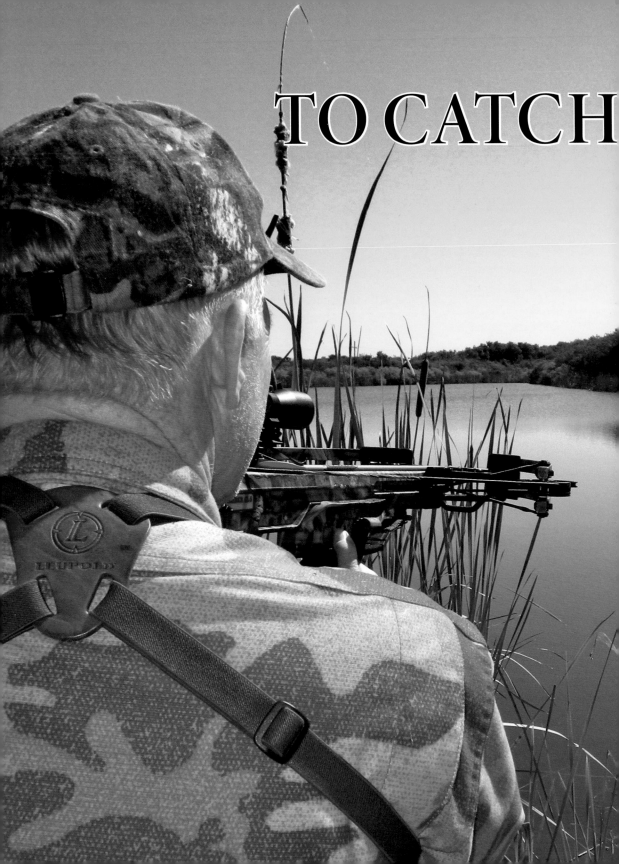

TO CATCH

A GATOR

CRAIG BODDINGTON

(IT'S NOT AS EASY AS IT SOUNDS.)

THE FINE GRAVEL was blistering hot as we slowly crawled along the levee, picking our way between fire ant mounds. The gator lay sunning on open sand on the far side of a canal. We'd glassed him at 500 yards, and he looked big. At 200 yards he looked huge . . . and that's when we ran out of cover and started crawling. Innate pessimism kicked in. I never gave us good odds of getting within crossbow range, but we had to try at least. At 100 yards we almost ran out of cover, but we kept crawling and the big lizard kept sleeping.

At 60 yards the weeds along the verge got taller. Suddenly it seemed we had a chance. We pitched up behind a leafy clump, 34 yards. Hoppy Kempfer set the sticks low for a sitting position, and I had the brain shot memorized. As I put the crossbow on the rest, the alligator slipped smoothly and silently into the canal. At least we got some exercise!

A GATOR COMEBACK

No, we're not talking about a Florida football game. Long pursued for its valuable leather, just a generation ago the American alligator was seriously threatened. Management works, and the recovery of the alligator—though rarely cited—may be one of our most successful conservation stories. Today

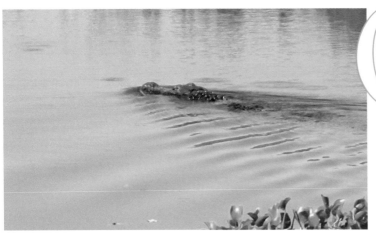

In the water a brain shot is the only option, but it takes a really experienced eye to judge an alligator from head size alone.

ONCE A GATOR STARTS MOVING, IT'S PRETTY MUCH ALL OVER.

there is some form of alligator harvest in all of our Gulf Coast states, and unlike our management policies for most native wildlife, there is an active (and well-managed) market for both skins and meat.

As we'll see, the hunting is a bit different, but today the alligator is properly recognized as a serious big-game trophy. I think that's good, but there are some anomalies. Like all reptiles, an alligator continues to grow throughout its (long) life . . . but growth slows with age. It doesn't take all that long to grow the medium-size gators that are most prized for leather. A good stretch of swamp habitat may hold dozens, if not hundreds, of purses, belts, and shoes in training. These are the gators that the commercial hunters all along the Gulf Coast are mostly looking for.

On the other hand, an outsider, whether he considers himself a "trophy hunter" or not, is probably looking for one big gator, call it a ten-footer or more. The alligator is not quite as big (and possibly not as aggressive a predator) as the crocodile.

The current Safari Club International record (Boone and Crockett doesn't recognize the alligator) is 14 feet 8 inches. That would be a big crocodile, but there are bigger. That's a huge alligator. An alligator of 12 feet, which is still a nice crocodile, is the Holy Grail. An 11-footer is outstanding, but that's now a very average crocodile. An alligator that breaks 10 feet is excellent.

Whether we're talking 10 footer or true monster, this is a different animal from the six- to eight-foot gators preferred—and commonly harvested—for skin and meat. Girth and weight increase along with length, but this takes time. A big gator is probably 60 or 70 years old . . . which means that it survived the time when its tribe was scarce. It has seen it all, has learned all the lessons man can teach it, and grown ever more wary with age.

THE SWAMP MONSTER

On the first day of my gator hunt with Osceola Outfitters' Hoppy Kempfer,

we penetrated thick cypress swamps looking for a hidden lagoon where a big gator had been seen. It took some looking—and we just about got penetrated by a cottonmouth in the process—but we found the lagoon and the big bull gator . . . along with a big female and a whole bunch of small fry.

The first time we saw him, he was fully exposed on a mud bar, seen through a screen of trees at maybe 100 yards. I have no experience with gators and don't pretend to be able to judge them, but Hoppy has taken hundreds, and he was excited. I do have some experience with crocodiles, and this gator would make a darn nice croc. Minimum 11 feet, maybe a bunch more . . . but he had found an ideal haven. Alligators, like crocodiles, have a full complement of senses. They smell, hear, and see extremely well. We could get the wind right and could find cover to conceal our approach, but the lagoon was surrounded by thick, noisy forest. And big alligators are always switched on. We approached his lagoon four times, and saw him four times, but there was no way we could close to crossbow range. We thought we had him every time, and then—just as we got into range —he dropped into the murky water and did not reappear.

More about techniques later, but we baited for him, using the regulation wooden plug. When we returned, the bait was taken, and the line led us to his cave at the far end of the lagoon. The location wasn't obvious, and now we understood why and how he had dropped below the surface and never came up for air. With a bit of luck we would have him; Hoppy and Jimmy Roseman on the line; me with the crossbow; Conrad Evarts behind me with the camera. It had the potential for the most exciting hunting video ever filmed. The line came in slowly, against much resistance. Bubbles came up . . . and then the line broke. And that, folks, was that. The cave, which this gator had excavated over decades, was clearly extensive, and we were out of options. He would regurgitate the plug and survive just fine. He might move, or he might stay put . . . but having spooked him this badly, we weren't going to see him again during the course of our hunt.

HUNTING OR FISHING?

Legal methods and licensing for alligators vary widely among the Gulf Coast states and may depend on where you're standing. In some situations, it really is more fishing than hunting. A trotline with hooks might be legal, thus just a matter of pulling the gator in then finishing him off with a revolver or "bang-stick"—or perhaps wrestling him to submission. On public land in Florida, neither hooks nor firearms can be used, although the previously described wooden plug—cut to very exact dimensions—is legal.

A couple of years ago, I hunted public waters in Florida with my friend and ace alligator hunter Nelson Lopez-Reyes. It was a real different deal! We hunted strictly at night with crossbow and harpoon arrow with line. I skipped an arrow off a big gator early on the first night, which can happen, but that was the only chance we got at a big one. We brought in a small gator shortly before dawn (legal cutoff) on the fourth night, and I was left with the impression that there was a whole lot more to this gator hunting than I'd realized!

On private lands in Florida, the game changes. There is no drawing for a permit. Landowners are issued permits in accordance with gator counts, and a visitor can assist in the harvest with an "agent" license. Methods of take also expand. Daylight hunting is legal, as are firearms. So you can hunt alligators exactly as crocodiles are hunted: stalking to certain rifle (or

bow) range, then taking the very difficult brain shot or the slightly simpler spine shot "behind the smile." Because you're working against allocated permits, you can "hunt" with a hook and a bang-stick. Our problem on the big gator I mentioned earlier was that we knew there were multiple gators in that lagoon, so although

A bait sack and floats. Wild hog killed on the property tastes great to man and gator alike.

perfectly legal, we couldn't use a hook for fear of the wrong gator taking the bait. (That gator was taken with a rifle on the next hunt, and he was every bit as big as Hoppy had thought.)

EVERY WHICH WAY

In a frenetic five days, we did it all. Hoppy Kempfer's family established the ranch in the 1890s, initially to harvest cypress timber. Cattle ranching remains a primary business, but in 1995 Hoppy began his commercial hunting operation, offering Osceola turkeys, Seminole whitetails, wild hogs, and, of course, alligators—all of which he has aplenty. I did a spring turkey hunt on a neighboring ranch maybe 25 years ago and shot a hog but didn't get a turkey, and at that time nonresident alligator hunting didn't exist. This was a different experience!

Turkey season had just ended, but we saw lots of turkeys and quite a few good gobblers. We saw lots of deer, but the bucks had dropped their antlers. What surprised me the most was the oceans of wild hogs! They could be found in major sounders mornings and evenings, and we encountered quite a few rumbling around at midday. We needed gator

bait, and an order was in for a couple of pigs for a barbecue, so I arrowed two with the Wicked Ridge with little difficulty. The Kempfer family has done a good job with their country, and there is lots of game.

There are also lots of gators, and we hunted them every which way. We stalked the swamp monster and several other big gators we glassed up along the levees. Taking a big one that way was far from impossible, but we were hunting with Wicked Ridge crossbows and had to get close. This is not easy, but as we hunters often do, we made a commitment to use certain equipment, and along with that comes limitations. At this writing, the big gator we stalked along that levee has not been taken. But if we were hunting with a rifle, we would have stopped around a hundred yards and had an easy shot.

Variations on the theme include calling. We were hunting during the primary mating season, late April, and a weird "chirping" call brought in several gators. They weren't big, but it could have happened that way as well.

ALMOST

We messed up on the beached whale, and we failed miserably on the swamp

A big gator is truly an awesome creature. A plus 10-footer like this is at least 60 or 70 years old, quite a different creature from the smaller gators preferred for commercial harvest.

monster. There were quite a few other stalks that went awry, and other tactics (like calling) that didn't work. But there were lots of gators—lots of big gators—so I genuinely believed it was only a matter of time. On a hot midday, it almost happened. There was a medium-sized pond adjacent to a levee, and it was full of croco ... excuse me, alligators. We pitched up there, glassing for bedded gators, and a very big head surfaced close to shore. I readied the crossbow, looking at a small oblong in the water. No way can I judge alligators from such a presentation, but Hoppy was sure this was a big one. So, offhand at 30 yards, quartering to me, I tried for the eye. I missed; the bolt skipped just over the top of his skull.

VICTORY AT SUNSET

Here's where the game changed. As with the swamp monster, it was no longer pure hunting but some combination of hunting and fishing. We knew this was a good gator, and we knew he was in this lagoon. We also knew the water held several other

Photo Credit: Mark Sidelinger

alligators of varying sizes. So we had no option but to bait with the wooden plug and hope the boss gator would take the bait before his little buddies got to it.

We baited the pond. When we came back a few hours later, all three floats were gone. We put a boat in and found one float on the far side, plug still attached but bait gone. The other two floats were in grass leading to an overgrown slough, a connection between the pond and a canal. This was not good. If he had gone into that tangled mess, there was no way we could get him out. That was pure speculation, because we didn't know if it was one gator or two or if there was anything on the end of either line.

Now the job was to pull the line in, slowly and carefully, hoping the plug didn't dislodge. The lines converged in a twisted tangle and came against resistance, almost certainly one gator. Then, instead of continuing up the slough, the lines turned and streamed out for open water. That was our big break. We definitely had a gator on— but how big?

He took us around the pond several times before we saw his head through the murky water. He looked big to me, and Hoppy confirmed it. I loaded the harpoon arrow and stood on the bow. As clumsy as I am, that was no small task—and I didn't want to go swimming with this thing! Then we went around some more, gaining and losing line, increasingly worried that he would spit out the plug. He came up splashing and snapping, and

Jimmy Roseman, Tenpoint Crossbows' Phil Bednar, Boddington, and Hoppy Kempfer with Boddington's sundown alligator.

I bounced the harpoon off his thick hide. Good Lord, this was crazy!

We lost line while I reloaded, but after a few more splashes and snaps, I planted the harpoon in the softer skin behind his jaw. Now we had him . . . or he had us. I reloaded with a broadhead, and the rodeo continued for several more minutes before I could get a clean shot at the brain. We dragged him onto a grassy bank just at sunset, not quite the biggest gator we'd seen, but a much bigger gator than I'd expected.

We spent the next day looking for a big hog and then went out that night to get Conrad a management gator. We switched roles: Conrad on the crossbow and me on the camera. I was perfectly happy about that. It was wild enough messing with one in daylight . . . but in the dark—totally nuts. Using the harpoon arrow and

lines, I'm still not sure if it's properly hunting or a bit more like fishing. But I've had few experiences so completely exciting! Ⓗ

To book your own hunt with Hoppy, visit —osceolaoutfitters.com

DYLAN FORSYTH

ROLLERCOASTER RAM

"...and there might be a legal ram in the group," Robin whispered, as he leaned in a bit to almost mumble the invaluable tidbit. A secret like this needed to be whispered, even though we were over three miles up the trail in a lonely valley. Robin had the look of a skinny Santa Claus—with a twinkle in his eye and a jolly smile—as he offered me the greatest gift of all.

I was hiking with my father-in-law, trying to fill his elk tag, when we ran into Robin. We were headed for home, but he was going back for another look at a band of bighorns he'd found several days before. I questioned his willingness to divulge such important information, but without saying much, he implied that he was holding out. My admiration for the man rose another level.

I've known Robin for several years. He is a neighbor who lives just a few houses away, and when I began my job in the electrical shop at the mine, he was finishing his career. My father-in-law had worked with him for nearly 30 years. He's in his late 50s, but he's still a true "gamer" when it comes to long, hard hikes into the wilderness. It's what he lives for.

I was vibrating from the information as we walked toward the truck. Prior commitments to my family and work meant I wouldn't be able to see for myself for at least a few days. I prayed Robin would get another look at the band of sheep and have the opportunity to decide for himself on the ram.

For three days I walked around in a trance, only one thing on my mind. Although I'd never killed a ram, I'd trekked countless miles over the last few years searching for a legal one. Unfortunately, Robin couldn't find the ram on that return trip. As I discussed my plans for my days off, he graciously offered to come along. I was ecstatic.

The next morning, as the dark lightened to gray, revealed a heavy, overcast sky. I was disheartened as we hiked into the backcountry, working our way up into a ceiling of fog. Regardless of the weather, we were committed to sticking it out. Robin spoke encouraging words throughout the morning, trying to ease my worries about the weather. His trusty companion Hank, a wire haired, lanky-legged dog, tried his best to refrain from yanking on the leash to chase birds. Robin seemed in his element as he packed in a scope, a tripod, water, and a few other items. I was glad to have their companionship for the hunt, and I focused on taking as much from the experience as I could. Killing a ram would simply be a bonus.

During the silent minutes in between short bursts of conversation, I drank in the experience. The smell of damp, almost frosty, pine forest filled my nostrils. My well-worn hiking boots felt like an extension of my legs. A small, repetitive squeak from my pack frame was only a minor annoyance as the sounds of our rhythmic footsteps working through the chorus of nature proved more interesting to my ears.

We made good time through the main valley and turned up a side draw. We'd gain elevation more rapidly now, and as I looked ahead, the ceiling of clouds seemed determined to not release the high ridges from its grip. We pushed forward anyway, glassing the bits of slope that we could see. It was still early, and there was a chance the clouds would lift enough to give us a better look.

Then, a silhouette materialized on the rocks above us. A quick glance through the binocular revealed only a banana ram, but it was a start. Scanning through the trees and the fluctuating clouds, we started to pick out several bodies, and it was soon apparent that we'd found the nursery. Fourteen ewes and three baby rams speckled the slope. Once we were satisfied with our count, we pushed on further up the valley.

It wasn't long before we saw another sheep silhouette bedded on the snowy face. Our blood started pumping as we stared at the big curls of a more mature ram. We settled in to the spotting scopes, straining to

HANK ENJOYS
ONE LAST MOMENT
OF RELAXATION
BEFORE THE LEASH
AND HARNESS
GO BACK ON FOR
THE PACK OUT.
☆ ☆ ☆ ☆ ☆ ☆ ☆

take every advantage the sky would give us. For half an hour we critiqued the biggest of the five rams but determined he needed to live a couple more years.

We took the opportunity to refuel with a drink and a tasty ram steak sandwich, compliments of Robin's sheep from the previous year. Looking around, we could see the clouds had lifted another 100 yards. We pushed on, methodically picking apart the steep walls to our left and right.

We had only gone a few hundred yards when I spotted another ram bedded up in a rocky, snowy draw. He was still young. But Robin's keen eye spotted a shape in the trees to the right. Our adrenaline spiked as we set up the scopes to glass the mature ram. Soon two rams appeared, then three, then four. The clutter kept us from judging any of them, but we knew there were a few mature rams in the band. One in particular got us very excited.

We waited patiently until the group finally filtered into the rocky draw the lone bedded ram occupied. The small ram got up and joined the group, making seven in total. Robin pulled out his Leica rangefinder and hit them at 330 yards. Our conversation focused on one particular ram broomed up on the left side. Our luck seemed to give out as the clouds began making the task of judging difficult. A fortunate glance gave me the impression that he was good.

Robin moved over to my big 80mm Swarovski scope and leaned into the eyepiece. Even through the binocular, I could tell he was a nice ram, but we wanted to be in total agreement. "I think he's a nice ram," I said. "If you want him, he's yours." Robin had spotted them first, and I wanted him to know he had first dibs on taking or passing up the ram.

As the band picked their way up the broken slope away from us, Robin's silence was excruciating. He finally broke the tension. "You'd better get your gun ready."

"Are you sure?" I asked? I was jittery.

"He's for you," he said. He shot them again with the rangefinder, but by this time it was reading 425 yards.

I debated the increased distance and the weather conditions. Looking at the terrain, and knowing I had my tripod to shoot on, I decided to take the shot rather than sneaking closer and possibly spooking them off. I've routinely shot to 450 yards and felt confident in my ability to make a lethal shot from that distance. I also felt the shakes settling in a bit from the reality of the situation: I was about to take a crack at my first ram.

I took time adjusting my tripod and settling in for a rest, as I wanted to calm down a bit before the shot. I cranked up my rifle scope to 15X, adjusted the focus, and concentrated on my breathing. After a few seconds, I indicated to Robin that it was time. I was really going to take a poke at a ram. As he peered through his binocular, spotting to see where my bullet would hit, I pulled the trigger... and pulled the shot high. As soon as the gun went off, I knew I had flinched.

A string of expletives erupted from my mouth. After all the work, all the preparation, and all the practice with

THE MOUNTAINSIDE WAS SO STEEP AND SLIPPERY THAT WE HAD TO TIE HIM OFF TO THE LAST TREE BEFORE HE WENT OVER AN UGLY CLIFF.

☆ ★ ☆ ★ ☆ ★ ☆ ★ ☆

Preseason scouting is crucial for success when hunting for a legal ram. High-end optics are imperative, not only for picking out animals, but for field judging as well.

my rifle, that is how I performed. To flinch and pull the shot while shooting at my first ram was crushing. I found the rams in my scope again and watched them race into the trees high up the ridge. My emotional rollercoaster ride hit a new low; it now felt more like a derailment. My glances bounced between my binocular and Robin as the sheep continued to climb the treacherous slope. His quiet, focused disposition had a calming effect and my frustration slowly waned. Robin glanced down at Hank and patted him on the head, "Don't worry, boy," he said. "We're gonna be having sheep tonight."

I was racked with indecision. What to do now? Do I wait and hope we could spot them through the fog?

Do I head up the hill after them? I raced back and forth, desperately trying to determine which side of the ridge the sheep might come out on. I also questioned whether they'd even come out of the trees. The worst part was questioning my own shooting ability. *If* I was fortunate enough to get a second chance, could I make it this time, or would I just miss again?

Finally, after half an hour of thought, I looked Robin in the eye. "I've gotta go after them," I said. "It's the only way to redeem myself." He smiled and nodded. We went over a couple quick hand signals to relay information while I was climbing after the sheep. We finished talking just as I slipped the mini-crampons over my boots. A

few deep breaths prepared me for the upcoming climb. More determined than ever, I set off and raced up the slope to reclaim my pride.

As taxing as the climb was on my body, my mind raced even faster than my heartbeat. I toiled to gain elevation into the clouds that rolled in and out. I glanced back at Robin to check my progress. The silence was broken by his deep voice echoing up the hillside. "They're cutting across to the right, way up," he yelled into the thin mountain air. "If you hurry, you might have a chance!" He stretched an arm high above his head, indicating the rams were moving above me.

I kicked it up a notch. I pushed the pain of burning lungs out of my mind. I forgot about my weakening legs. I only focused on redemption. I aimed my body for the hidden ridge that slowly opened up above me and to the right. I tried my best to remain as positive as I could throughtout the climb. It was hard, though, because my mind kept allowing this negative thought to creep in: I might never catch up with them.

A glance into the last bit of trees dismissed that thought as a ram emerged from the stunted, alpine cover. A flicker glowed on the candle of hope. I hit the turf and tried to range the ram. No reading. I tried again, but the fog wouldn't let it happen. I gave up trying to get a reading on the ram's location and ranged a tree below him on the slope: 256 yards. I guessed the ram at 300 yards and dialed up my scope for another shot.

Laying prone, I glanced through the short pine trees and saw parts of two other rams, but the fog wouldn't allow me to determine their size.

Once we caped the ram and slid his carcass to a flatter area, we could finally breathe a sigh of relief and enjoy a second round of field photos. Notice the small horn-like growth on the bridge of his nose.

Time was running out. Frustration set in again as I felt the pain of the cold snow around me and felt my chance at redemption slowly slip away. Any minute the rams would walk deep into the trees or fade into the fog.

After 10 minutes, the sky cooperated and lifted a bit, revealing five rams on the slope. I tried to take the opportunity to glass them through my binocular, but they were filled with snow. Dropping them, I raised my riflescope, but now it was fogged over. Time was ticking. I cleaned off the scope and judged the band. But the ram I wanted was missing. I desperately scanned the surrounding area and spotted another body. Before I could get a good look, the clouds rolled over again, and this time they dumped a layer of snow.

By this time I was all but beat, physically and mentally drained. The flicker of hope was dying. I wondered at what point I should give up. But then the clouds lifted to reveal a sixth ram. I dumped the fresh snow from my scope and focused on him. It was yet another disappointment for me. He was short. Minutes passed by slowly as I waited for an opportunity to glimpse the seventh, and final, ram.

Looking up the steep slope, I spotted another wave of snow clouds rolling towards me. I had time for one last glance at the group; one last count of the band. One, two, three, four, five, six... seven! A head poked out from behind a small pine. Anxious moments passed, then the perfect look presented itself. I knew instantly it was the ram I was after. The sky was closing in; I couldn't wait any longer. It was now or never.

With only the front portion of the shoulder visible, I threaded the needle. The shot felt perfect. I felt calm. The ram buckled on the boom of my .300. It was over. A weight lifted from my body, and I let out a holler that risked an avalanche. It was answered by a holler from Robin. It was a truly indescribable feeling.

Twenty minutes later, the last bit of anxiety left me as I approached the downed ram. Wading through the thigh deep snow, it took only a quick glance to know he was a beautiful, full-curl ram. I had finally redeemed myself. Robin and Hank worked their way up and met me next to the fallen monarch.

I looked in admiration at the 58-year-old man who had inspired my drive and with whom I credited my success. Most importantly, Robin was the man that reminded me the experience, not the animal, was the ultimate prize in hunting. His anxiety, while spotting from down below, had matched mine, but his smile showed that his happiness and satisfaction also surpassed mine.

Robin gave me a ram, but more importantly, he gave me a glimpse into a level of emotions I'd never felt hunting. He has shown me the highs and lows of sheep hunting. I don't know if I can offer the same generosity Robin displayed. The best thing I can do is pass on his vision of the experience to others. And keep passing it on. Ⓗ

ILLUSTRATIONS by
DOUG SHERMER

BIG

STUFF

MIKE LUNENSCHLOSS

The other day I did something, mercifully, I almost never do. I stumbled on, and read, one of those online hunting forums. The advice that was given in a particular thread was reckless, downright injurious, to the point of possibly being fatal.

A fellow requested advice on which rifle to buy for a brown bear hunt, a .416 or a .375 H&H. Many said you cannot go wrong with either. Having collected both grizzly and brown bear with each, no more accurate statement could have been tendered. Disturbingly, several of these online experts advocated much more junior calibers. Acknowledging the calibers' inadequacy, they assured the readers "a guide will be there to back you up."

Having been charged by both coastal brown and interior grizzly bears, I have been schooled that they can come at you with all the warning of a lightning strike. The world's largest carnivore does not need the excuse of being wounded to charge. Every year a sample of unarmed people take up residence in Alaskan hospitals after having been mauled by an unprovoked bear. This is to say if one is going to hunt bear, one should possess marksmanship skills and a rifle capable of humanely handling such situations yourself. The guide may be at the creek getting water or visiting the loo, in which case he may only have a roll of toilet paper in his hand to back up the hunter.

Of course, you recognize that well enough. You, avid hunters and readers of this magazine, find the notion of planning a hunt that would require the guide shooting your game inconceivable. The point being all this thinking of toilet paper, a brown bear charging, and .375 H&H and .416s brought back the memory of a past hunt. Truth is stranger than fiction, as is commonly reported, and the account of this hunt, though undeniably strange, is true to the minutest detail.

Reading this magazine, it is easy to develop the impression that big-game hunts in Alaska, Africa, and Canada are all concluded magnificently. Our sport's most prolific author always brings handsome trophies to hand with skill and ease. However, I will stop short of mentioning Craig Boddington by name for I have a healthy dose of respect for his depth of knowledge. My hunts, on the extreme other hand, are fraught with bad weather, bad food, the worst of luck, and something few admit to: I do, on rare occasions, miss most disgracefully.

As you well know, in the elements of a successful hunt, area and outfitter are of cardinal importance, and Mel Gillis on the Alaska Peninsula receives my highest marks. Mel, who never met a cigar he didn't like, towers at six feet five and is as honest as he is Texas-tall. My guide, Jeff Hirsch, has a deserved reputation from Kodiak to the Brooks Range of being able to size a bear to within a couple of inches from a mile away.

Knowing Jeff and his distinguished reputation, I had requested him. It was not the first time I had done so, nor would it be the last. At Mel's base camp, arriving from Kodiak Island, Jeff squirmed out of the back seat of a Super Cub and stretched in hunting clothes that hung on him in chaos. The mismatched laces on his worn-out hunting boots lacked the discipline of a knot. As he pulled out his raingear, I noticed it was not the breathable Gore-Tex type but closer to boiler plate, the standard issue worn by commercial fishermen on the Bering Sea. His patched hip boots had been chest waders before he had taken his skinning knife to them. With the notable exceptions of a .416 Remington and well-worn 10X binoculars of the highest quality, he had no other gear. His only clothes were on his back, where they had been for the last 30 some days. The thought of regularly changing, or washing, even so much as his socks had never occurred to him. As we once again shook hands, a genuine smile cracked from beneath a month's worth of filmy grime.

"Jeff, you still single?"

"Yeah, too young and beautiful to be married," he replied.

After a few moments to sort out ten days of food, we began helping pilots Tom Atkins and Carl Brent load their Super Cubs as they rocked in the ever present wind rolling in off Bristol Bay. In no time the snow-covered, volcanic spine of the Alaska Peninsula was slowly passing beneath us. Our destination was one of the many nameless drainages found on the east face. Final approach came too soon as we lined up for a speck innocent of alders, a rare find. Though heavily loaded, our Cubs floated down as though they were lighter than my wallet. As soon as the tundra tires rolled out on the surface for which they were named, we set up spike camp: two tents, one for our minimal gear and food, the other for sleeping. In those tight quarters, at the end of the day when Jeff pulled off his boots, believe me, it was intense.

We were up early, but never able to make it by first light at that time of year. An hour of glassing, then breakfast, hours more of glassing, a lunch break, more glassing. Dinner was always a welcome respite and more entertaining than nourishing as Jeff chewed his

food with half the teeth he was originally issued—a silent testimony to his toughness in pugilistic endeavors. No dessert on this menu, as our dizzied eyes scoured the hills for a brownie until ten. As a kid, glassing for big game always seemed so glamorous as I read about it at the magazine rack in the corner pharmacy, but after a few days of this routine you have had enough.

Bears materialized on all points of the compass, but none of the 10-foot-plus variety until the eighth day. Before breakfast Jeff had spotted a large sow in the company of a boar, busily engaged in courtship of the bruin bombshell. Breakfast now forgotten, we were rifled up and after him as we pulled up our hip boots. It was painstakingly slow work as we fought our way upslope through a sea of alders so thick the range of vision was measured in feet not yards. Had we not been driven on by the prospect of collecting a monster, this route would scarcely have been regarded as penetrable.

"Mike, you got any toilet paper I can borrow? I just crapped my pants." To which I replied:
"Borrow?"

To a tourist, the Alaskan alders always seem comfy and garden pleasant. Only distance can offer such enchantment. This beguiling deception an experienced hunter never falls for. To hunters, the sight of alders foretells of unspeakably wicked travel, preferably up a tumbling stream that has scoured some degree of thinning.

The next morning Jeff walked up returning my long johns. . . .

"That's OK, Jeff, you may keep them ...think of it as your tip."

After an hour of this unpleasant exercise, Jeff stopped and turned to me, asking, "Mike, you got any toilet paper I can borrow? I just crapped my pants."

To which I replied: "Borrow???"

Fearing fighting such demons myself, I did have some, given to him without hesitation, and with the clear understanding he was not to return it. Try enduring the consequences of eight straight days of Tex-Mex lasagna yourself and such an episode will hardly seem remarkable.

Topping the ridge, we found this knoll to be for bears what an ant hill is to ants. Trails crisscrossed in and out of the alders. These are not game trails, rather centuries old footprints from the largest carnivores since the dinosaur. For a thousand years they retraced their exact steps, leaving ruts in the gravelly Alaska soil.

Almost immediately, our wandering stalk came to a halt to allow crossing traffic, an eight-foot bear right to left. Then it happened with the surprise of a sneeze: the stately procession we were hoping for commenced. A 9½-foot sow majestically treads across an opening with our 10-foot boar in tow. Given she is truly one of the most fearsome creatures to ever roam the planet, it is no small feat to create an illusion of dwarfing a 9½-foot brown bear. However, the massive 10-foot male had 30 percent more body weight, making the sow appear petite.

With my .375 H&H now at my shoulder and the crosshairs on the bear's shoulder, there was no time for admiration as we heard a colossal racket from our left. It was unmistakable: another brown bear charging at a surprising pace through the very alders that had given us such grief.

"Damn, that is aggressive, a bear charging on scent," I thought. At 30 yards he burst from the alders and slowed. However, this unprovoked ferocity did not end there. With a scowling cruelty that only a human mother-in-law could match, the bear paced back and forth, snapping his teeth. Why he stopped rather than driving the charge home is anyone's guess, but my money is on the fact he got a good whiff of Jeff.

With this unexpected complication, we cursed our luck accordingly and waited for the ill-tempered demon to retreat before making another stalk on the bigger boar, now hidden somewhere in the alders. However, with unrelenting vocal threats of a most unpleasant intensity, this new challenger clearly had persistence worthy of a more noble pastime.

Jeff, in a steady, clear tone that acknowledged there was no need to whisper, said, "Let's move," and we slipped away to our right on a bear trail through an alder patch. After all, the bear, still pacing in a fit of rage, had rendered hopeless a stalk on any animal that was not stone deaf.

As we crept away, I did so looking over my shoulder with my .375 at the ready. Suddenly, I crashed into Jeff. Unbeknownst to me, my guide had stopped dead and now stood as still as a statue. A regard for truth forbids me from testifying that we looked like anything other than Laurel & Hardy as the aforementioned eight-footer rose up and blocked our path.

Full of conjecture as to the intentions of this beast, I snapped the Mauser up should emergency action be required. Despite the best glass money could buy, at that proximity nothing but out of focus hair was visible in the scope. Within the choked confines of the trail Jeff leaned against me as the bear, not thinking it polite to molest us, ambled aside at a pace that could only be described as full leisure. We then stepped off 11 comfortable steps to where he had stood, on his hind feet, eyeing us attentively. We humans can claim no monopoly on curiosity; when an animal indulges in it such behavior often proves to be his demise, but not for this youngster... not this time.

We trolled around in vain, straining to renew our acquaintance with the 10-foot boar until the May Alaska sun began to exhaust its strength. It had been a gripping day in which sweat, and adrenalin, had flowed freely, but

not so much as a morsel had been eaten to modify our discomfort in the chill of evening. As a breeze bowled down from the snowcapped peaks, I found myself being refrigerated in sweat-soaked gear, but I had to be more contented in my kit than Jeff was in his.

Not so much as an utterance of a complaint from Jeff. As a matter of fact, the only thing he said to me was: "When we get back to base camp don't tell Mel I didn't convince you shoot that second 9½ footer. He'll have me out in the shed with my head in a vise."

Certainly, one could call himself no poorer for having collected such a fine trophy, but it is hard to settle on one animal when the Goliath you truly want could be behind the next excuse for a tree.

There was yet another encounter with a brown as we began our 10 p.m. descent, but it amounted to nothing.

Upon reaching our tent camp, Jeff walked with purpose to the creek to wash the diabolical discharge from his pants. My offer of a new pair of long underwear while his

dried was enthusiastically accepted. The next morning Jeff walked up returning my long johns, after having slept in their luxury.

"That's OK, Jeff, you may keep them."

"You sure, Mike?"

I replied in a moment of humor during an otherwise serious conversation. "Yeah, Jeff, think of it as your tip."

Such is the kidding in camp; in reality, I yield to no one in respect for this man.

Since then, Jeff bought the old P&T guiding area on Kodiak Island, famous from the book *Last of the Great Brown Bear Men.* He guided that storied concession for years, then sold it. He went to the Alaska State Fair, in Palmer, where he bought a solitary lottery ticket—not just any ticket, the winning ticket.

Jeff called me just the other day. He was making a short stop in Alaska before heading to Hawaii for more of his new passion, fighting sailfish with rod and reel. Seems he now finds shorts more comfortable than hip boots. ⓗ

Be a Shot Caller

Calling your shot will make you a deadlier and more effective hunter.

Guide Hagen Watkins, peering through Trijicon's TA11 ACOG atop DPMS's Lite Hunter in .308 Win., gets ready to call his shot on a South Texas whitetail.

My first deer rifle was a Post-'64 Winchester Model 70 in 7mm Mauser. Rather than shoot low-pressure (and low-recoil) factory 7x57 ammo, however, we shot my uncle's handloads, which fired 140-grain Noslers at just under 2,800 fps. The load proved to be supremely effective at two things: killing game and kicking the snot out of my shoulder. (I'm a recoil wuss now; imagine what I was like as a 70-pound kid.)

We all know recoil lays the foundation of the dreaded flinch, and I can honestly say that rifle gave me a gnarly one. But I must admit that two good things came from my early battles with recoil: I learned to call my shots and I learned how to cycle firearms very quickly (because I often missed); both skills have helped immensely in my hunting career.

So what is "calling the shot"? Calling the shot is simply remembering the exact sight picture the moment your rifle fires. As we begin to take up trigger pressure moments before firing, our brain is constantly analyzing and adjusting our sight picture to hit a precise spot on the target. At the shot, our brain "snaps" an image of the sight picture the moment we lose it in recoil. Remembering this final image allows us to predict with reasonable confidence where that projectile will impact the target only milliseconds after firing.

Calling the shot is important for two reasons. The first is when we're sighting-in at the range. Calling the shot here will confirm if an errant shot was our fault or the fault of the rifle/load. The second reason to call the shot is for follow-up shots at game. If the shot felt decent and the last image looked good, there may not be a reason to put another bullet into a staggering deer that is literally dead on its feet. However, if the shot felt OK but the last image indicated a bad shot (e.g., gutshot or lower leg hit), then the shooter will know to quickly put another bullet in the wounded animal.

Many of us already call our shots, but for those that don't, it's not hard to learn. Rimfire and dry-fire practice is the easiest way to develop or enhance your skills. Be sure to work on squeezing the trigger until its break surprises you. A surprise trigger break is always better than a jerked one. Also, be sure to keep your eyes open until after recoil occurs. Many shooters unknowingly shut their eyes when they pull the trigger, making it impossible to call the shot.

I was recently reminded the importance of this practice on a whitetail cull hunt in South Texas with Mellon Creek Outfitters (melloncreekoutfitters.com). They have an incredible number of deer that roam the immense, free-range property. "Too many, in fact," said Dustin Mueller, the ranch manager of Mellon Creek. "In order to increase the overall health of the herd, we need

to kill a lot of deer. Even with 110,000 acres of premium habitat, there's only so much food to go around."

So over the course of three days, a small group of us braved the 90-degree heat and 100-percent humidity and traipsed the dense mesquite thickets and salt grass meadows that teemed with rattlesnakes and wild hogs and helped cull as many of the ranch's estimated 6,000 whitetails as we could. This opportunity to shoot a lot of deer allowed me to pay close attention to my shooting. In country where deer are only a few steps away from thick foliage, calling the shots proved critical for quick recovery, as the heat forced us to field dress and cool the animals as quickly as possible to avoid spoilage.

As we were heading back to camp one morning, a fat doe scampered across the road and paused before heading into a mesquite patch. I settled the glowing dot of my Trijicon AccuPoint behind her shoulder, and my DPMS barked a 62-grain bullet. The deer took off into the thicket like it was unhurt. My guide truly thought I had missed, but I knew better. As our five-minute search became 15 minutes, I, too, started to wonder, but I kept recalling my mental sight picture at the time of recoil. It had to be a good hit, I thought. Sure enough, it was. The doe was piled up less than 20 yards from where she was hit. We just hadn't travelled far enough down the road to find her.

They say practice makes perfect. So next time you go out shooting, whether at the range or in the field, pay close attention to your sight picture at the time of the shot. Being able to call the shot and know where your bullet will hit may transform the outcome of a future hunt from piss-poor to picture-perfect. ⓗ

LOOK, MA, NO BATTERIES!

My favorite optics for calling the shot are scopes with glowing reticles, such as the Trijicon AccuPoint I recently used in Texas. In the same way a laser sight makes coaching a pistol shooter so much easier, a lighted reticle makes it easier to call the shot, as the bright aiming point seems to burn into our last mental image before recoil occurs. What makes the AccuPoint line noteworthy is that it uses fiber optics and radioactive tritium to illuminate the aiming point. It's completely battery free and available in four models: 1-4x24, 3-9x40, 2.5-10x56, and 5-20x50. *$927–1,350; trijicon.com*

Bowhunting Big Cats

Think you're prepared to face a mountain lion with a stick and string? Think again.

Photo Credit: Mike Schoby

Several years ago, the hounds were unleashed on a track south of Salt Lake City, Utah, at dawn, and by noon we'd treed six mountain lions. No doubt the fresh snow and favorable winds created excellent conditions for tracking that day, but the fact is, the Western U.S. is crawling with big cats. If you're interested in one of the most adventurous hunts offered in the Lower 48, now's a great time to book. Soon after you commit, the conversation between you and your outfitter will turn to your physical condition and your weaponry.

Frankly, mountain lion hunting is all about the chase—chasing the dogs as they chase the cat hell-bent over and through places that might be impossible if it weren't for the adrenaline and the guide's encouragement to save his dogs. If the dogs tree and the cat cooperates, the actual kill can be anti-climactic. The shot is normally close and technically easy. Contrary to nonsense floating around on feline-lover forums, cats assuredly do not have more than one life. What a mountain lion does have are two lungs, a heart, and a spot-on impression of Edward Scissorhands should you tickle him in the wrong area. Mountain lions are not natural-born terrors, like leopards that prefer nothing more than raking the guts out of humans if prodded; in fact, they are usually rather timid. Nonetheless, hunters should realize that if you wound any big cat, you could have more to wrestle than just a sick feeling in your stomach.

The average male lion weighs 140 pounds, or slightly less than a mature whitetail. Therefore, penetration with any modern compound bow, arrow, and broadhead combination north of 250 feet per second is not an issue. At first blush you may think arrow speed is desirable to mitigate string jumping—after all, cats have superior reaction times. But consider that the likely scenario you'll encounter is one where the cat is in a tree. It'll either be lying on a branch, acting like it couldn't be more relaxed while the dogs raise hell below, or hissing-mad and trying to bore through your skull with its fiery yellow eyes. Either way, there'll be plenty of noise and chaos, so the lion is unlikely to notice the subtle thunk of a bowstring.

What are major issues, however, are the in-the-tree shot scenario, legality and durability of equipment, and preparation.

BROADHEADS

Scott and Angie Denny, owner/operators of Table Mountain Outfitters, are based out of Wyoming but hunt lions in Idaho. Over the years, their clients have taken over 50 cats, 25 percent of which were taken with a bow.

What is primarily important to Table Mountain is making sure hunters comply with individual state game laws. The mechanical vs. fixed-blade debate continues in Wyoming, but some states, like Idaho, have outlawed mechanicals. Where mechanicals are allowed, though, any of the ultra-sharp two- and three-blade heads are adequate. The Rage Hypodermic is deadly, especially now that Rage has improved its rear-

Hunting behind dogs adds another thrill to the already nerve-racking chase in big cat country. The hunt can be just as dangerous for the dogs as it is for their owners. Photo Credit: Mike Schoby

deploying blade heads with a locking collar instead of an O-ring. NAP's Killzone is an excellent mechanical, as is the company's three-blade Spitfire.

Because most cougars are shot out of trees, however, shooting lanes cannot be planned. Many times an archer must thread an arrow through branches, and this can especially be a problem for mechanical heads. My testing has revealed that most mechanicals will deploy prematurely if they come into contact with anything before reaching the target, and if a blade deploys while in flight it becomes wildly inaccurate. Of course, fixed blades will also deflect, but they will usually not lose balance and wind-plane to the extent of a mechanical. For this reason, and the fact that a big cat is potentially

dangerous, I believe the best choice of broadheads are tried-and-true fixed blades, like Muzzy, NAP Thunderhead and Hellrazor, and G5 Montec.

SHOT PLACEMENT

As always, shot placement trumps all, and since a cat's heart and lungs are placed farther forward and slightly lower than deer, a quartering away shot placed low (to account for the heart and the typical extreme angle when shooting into a tree) is ideal. Be sure to think in three dimensions while envisioning the placement of the orange-sized heart suspended in the chest. It's not uncommon to aim at the cat's pectoral muscle, so the arrow goes up through the chest and exits between the back of the neck and shoulder. Usually, you will have a moment to walk around the tree and find a desirable angle. As soon as you and the guide decide it's time to shoot, slowly move around the tree

to find it—avoiding eye contact with the cat—and take the shot. Remember to draw, anchor, then bend back at the waist rather than merely moving your draw arm up. This technique mitigates changes in point of impact.

DURABILITY

"When hiking into any tree in a typical mountain lion scenario, you need to protect your sight and sight pins," Angie said. "We have trouble with people catching their sights on brush and ripping the pins out."

So buy a tough, all-metal sight and, make sure the bolts are secured with Loctite. If it has plastic fiber-optic pins, make sure they just illuminate the metal pins and do not form the pins themselves. Also, consider buying or making a protective cover for your sight, like the bowsight cover offered by Cabela's. For an added measure of insurance, make reference marks on your bow with a Magic Marker. Outline your sight on your riser, and then mark your pin positions on your sight so you can quickly see if the sight pins or the sight itself has been moved. Most importantly, make sure your broadheads are secured and covered before chasing after the dogs.

FINAL THOUGHTS

There is a mountain lion stalking a deer as you read this, and by December you could be stalking him over the wildest country you've ever imagined. Get in the best shape of your life, grab your bow, and prepare for the hairiest, snarlingest, highest-pressure easy shot you've ever taken. Ⓗ

SUPER
GRADE

JOSEPH VON BENEDIKT

ELK

EVERY AMERICAN HUNTER HAS A GREATEST MOMENT IN MEMORY

IT WAS ALMOST midday, and the unforgiving high-altitude sun had already forced me to pause and shrug out of my pack and orange vest in order to peel off a layer of the wool that had protected me against the morning's penetrating cold. Amos, my grizzled, taciturn guide (whose parents, I was becoming convinced, had somehow crossbred with elk), stopped in the fringe of trees at the bottom of a meadow and wisely waited for me to disrobe and reassemble my cooler self before raising his cow call.

THE

heat and blazing sun didn't inspire confidence, but instantly, a gritty, aggressive bugle floated down from a half-mile up the timbered ridge beyond the meadow. Amos grinned and whispered, "Maybe we'll stop here for lunch."

I barely had time to conjure up an image of the sandwich and multiple chocolate bars in my pack when another angry, demanding bugle ripped across the meadow. Same bull, but this time he was much closer.

Amos's eyebrows leapt to his hairline. "He's coming!" he hissed, trying not to sound surprised as he faded into the brush. Finding a good field of fire into the meadow above, I settled against an aspen trunk and ran a .300 H&H cartridge into the chamber of the pre-war, pre-'64 Winchester Model 70 Super Grade.

Without doubt, I was on the best elk hunt of my life.

Deep in the belly of one of northern Utah's high canyons, I was hunting a controlled wildlife management unit (CWMU) with Jason Hornady. From the first pre-light dawn several days ago, when I'd stepped from Amos's pickup into a land of elk-enchantment, the sound of bugling bulls had rung incessantly around me. We were hunting an old-age class of bulls—eight years or above—and had passed on innumerable big bulls in the days since.

By my best count, I was looking at 15 to 20 6x6 or better bulls per day—elk nirvana. We'd seen three bulls that I dearly wanted to shoot, but which were too young; I'd passed on several that were old enough but just not quite the right bull; and I'd blown one chance of a lifetime at smell-the-bull distance in thick timber.

ON VAST, LOW-PRESSURE AREAS MANAGED FOR HIGH BULL-TO-COW RATIOS AND OLD-AGE-CLASS BULLS, ELK HUNTING IS OF ANOTHER WORLD ENTIRELY.

GEARED UP

When Jason extended the invitation to hunt that part of Utah, I knew better than most what a blessed opportunity it was, as I'd been trying to draw a similar tag in my native Utah for 15 years.

Preparation was a joyful agony. What to hunt with? Out of respect to Jason (and because I heartily love the company's products), I would hunt with Hornady bullets. But what rifle? What gear? A profoundly addicted elk nut, I've hunted most of the Western states and used everything from ragged military surplus camo during my lean college years to cutting-edge fabrics in the latest evolution of hunting wear, but this hunt was different. Every elk hunt is special, but this one...this one was beyond special.

For whatever reason, the throwback in me laid claim to the hunt. I set aside the high-tech fabric and packed Levi's and checkered Pendleton shirts (which is what I wear every day anyway), my Filson wool coat, along with my Browning Full Curl Wool. I contacted my old shooting mentor, the man who taught me the finer points of competitive shooting, and begged the loan of a rifle I'd coveted for decades: the pre-'64, pre-war Winchester Model 70 Super Grade in .300 H&H that his father had given him.

Not to be fanatical about going retro, I mounted a brand-new Zeiss Conquest HD5 3-15X 42mm scope with the uber-capable Rapid-Z 800 ballistic reticle on the rifle and carried a Swarovski EL Range binocular.

THE ULTIMATE TROPHY TAG

ELK ARE A PART of life in the Rockies. Preferred to mule deer by most for its large-fibered, mild meat, elk are the pinnacle of readily achievable game. Most states have obtainable tags, either for OTC purchase or available in a high-percentage draw. Those tags offer residents a chance to hunt, and if they hunt hard and smart, a reasonable chance of bringing home winter meat.

Read enough Western "journal of my hunt" type magazines, and you'll get a sense of the excitement when a lucky middle-aged fellow draws a tag he's been putting in for since he legally could.

Drawing such an elk permit is a very big deal indeed and generally puts the lucky hunter into an area—public or private—that is managed for an almost-untouched population with very high bull-to-cow ratios and old-age class of bulls.

In many states, participating landowners with a large amount of private land within the borders of trophy elk management units are obligated to allow a certain amount of tag-drawing hunters to hunt on their property each fall but are, in recompense, given transferable landowner tags. Some use the tags themselves, but their considerable worth prompts most to sell the tags. In my native Utah, such private-land areas are called CWMUs.

A key point to these landowner-type tags: In many states hunters may purchase one without losing the preference points they've been accumulating for years.

Frankly, in many states landowner tags are so expensive that only hunters with plenty of spare change can afford them. Outdoorsmen excluded by finances sometimes view the system with a bitter eye. However, it's worth keeping perspective: Where healthy populations of game favor a landowner financially, the landowner tends to protect and promote healthy populations. I've never been anywhere near capable of affording a

landowner trophy elk tag, but that doesn't change the appreciation I have of how the system has brought areas of the West back to frontier-like elk population demographics.

In addition, some states' systems benefit blue-collar hunters, too. Many of the bulls I've shot in Utah were on "spike-only" tags, used for population control in big public-land trophy units and available over the counter. Inexpensive even for nonresidents, such tags offer hunters the opportunity to hunt thriving elk populations with a decent chance of shooting an ideal meat bull.

I have somewhere north of 15 points toward a trophy bull tag on my home unit in southern Utah, and statistically, it will be another three to six years before I have a better-than-even chance to draw the hunt I want.

After I do draw the lucky tag and shoot a bull, I'll have a five-year waiting period before I can begin applying again. By then, there will be thousands of hunters with upwards of 25 or 30 points ahead of me.

With all that information as background, you'll understand just how flabbergasted and delighted I was to be invited to hunt a legendary CWMU in northern Utah last fall. And the hunt was just as spectacular as I'd hoped.

If you dream of elk, apply. Pick a state—preferably your home state if you live in the West—and put in for the draw every year. Yes, it will take you a while to obtain a tag, but the dollars you spend applying each year benefit wildlife conservation, and when you finally pull that prized tag, you'll be in for an unforgettable elk hunt of a lifetime.

Initially, the .300 H&H gave lackluster accuracy, but my old friend had promised that it was superbly accurate. Armed with a good quantity of once-fired brass from the rifle's chamber, I tried handloading and struck paydirt with my first load.

Pushing a Hornady 180-grain InterBond bullet ahead of 69 grains of Reloder 19 powder, the rifle produced 2,935 fps and shot well. After shooting 1.5-inch and smaller groups at 200 yards, I ran a calculation on Zeiss's Rapid-Z reticle support site, dialed the scope's magnification to the suggested setting, and settled in for a shot at my 500-yard steel torso target. With my wife watching through a spotting scope, I fired and rang the steel, leaving a lead smear a hair above center. The second shot smacked two inches above the first. I fired again, and before the sound of the shot had faded, my wife said, "You're going to like this!"

All three shots had impacted within a 2.5-inch group.

At that distance the InterBond would still be carrying over 2,170 fps and 1,883 ft.-lbs. of energy at my home elevation, and clearly had adequate accuracy to cleanly drop a bull. I was ready.

INTO THE TIMBER

Literally within minutes of first setting foot in our hunting area, we worked in on and watched a beautiful 6x6 bull in thick timber—a bull you'd strain a gut to shoot on almost any other elk hunt. "Too young," whispered Amos.

Later another young bull—I'm guessing five or six—stood up from where he'd been bedded only 40 yards from us. Tremendous royal tines and

After zeroing—and shooting 1.5-inch groups at 200 yards—this 2.5-inch, three-shot group was fired from 500 yards using Zeiss's Rapid-Z 800 ballistic reticle.

whale tails towered, and although his lower tines were not extraordinary, my hunt would have been over right then had Amos not given me the evil eye. The genetics of the area are outstanding—that young bull had length, mass, everything that makes for a super-bull except age.

By the middle of the second afternoon, we'd looked at so many bulls that they were beginning to fade into a blur, a kaleidoscope of elk mixed inseparably. I'd gotten over the flush of eagerness, become steady, almost complacent, about viewing new bulls. Perhaps that's partly why I screwed up on an extraordinary bull when we found him.

In the early evening we worked through thick timber down the north face of a long east/west ridge and had already bumped, looked at, and passed on several mature bulls when we emerged noisily into a tiny half-acre opening on the steep hillside. So deep and harsh that it vibrated in

my ribcage, a bugle rang out from the patch of aspen saplings at the head of the opening. A shockingly wide rack pushed through the saplings toward us, inquisitive. I whipped the Winchester off my shoulder, my mind noting like slides in a black-and-white show the bull's obscenely long brow tines and thirds and the club-like mass of his main beams.

At that point, I didn't need approval. The Rapid-Z crosshair found the quartering-to bull's shoulder just as his head swung sideways, revealing that he was a 5x5. I paused.

Second-guessing myself, I shifted a half-step toward Amos and whispered under my breath, "He's only a five-point."

"We've been trying to get that bull for three years," he replied. Smart enough to evaluate him through my scope instead of my binoculars, in case I needed to shoot fast, I

The author pauses for a moment to calm his nerves and soak in the moment before approaching his bull, which lay in thick pines nearby.

A forester when not guiding, Amos is more elk than human. Few callers can consistently fool today's call-wise bulls; **Amos is one of them.**

shouldered the rifle again, and in a whisper of movement the bull was gone, swallowed into the saplings like smoke in the wind, leaving only the memory of massive, longer-than-possible lower tines, steeple-tall and beer-can thick royals, andlong, sweeping main beams lacking a fifth tine. That and a heartsick, sinking feeling in me.

I had him dead to rights, centered in my crosshairs at only 40 yards, I'd let my need for the classic 6x6 bull skew my judgment at the last second and had lost a bull that carried the frame of a 370- or 380-class monster. So what if he scored "only" 340 or 350 because he lacked fifth tines?

That night was the most action-packed yet, and I had the safety off on a great 330-class bull that Amos clearly thought I should shoot right at dusk. But his lower tines were short and stubby, and

Taking a bull like this may well be a once-in-a-lifetime experience. The author's vintage side exerted sway, and he hunted clad in wool, with a superb old Winchester Model 70.

the memory of the monster 5x5 and the knowledge that I had three days left stilled my hand. We hiked out in full dark, bugles ringing around us as we worked up the canyon through wallow-ridden meadows.

Weather blew in the third day, and we found and again passed on a bull that had cranked my heartrate the first day—a narrow but tall, colorful 7x7 with great, long S-shaped inline "cheaters" sweeping out from the base of his royal tines. Borderline too

young. "Maybe eight, but I think he's only seven," said Amos.

I'd have pressed, suggesting another look, but we'd caught a glimpse of a heavy bull, alone, feeding up the bottom of a finger tributary, and his occasional bugle rasped a clarion invitation across the canyon like some prehistoric moan. We left the 7x7 and followed. The bull was old, all right. Close, 90 yards close, we sat screened by scrub oak and watched. Drawn to a skeleton from rutting too hard for his age, he'd finally

Still in his prime at an estimated 11 years of age, the author's bull had unusual dewclaws on all four hooves—for whatever reason they hadn't worn off; long and curling almost like tiny sheep's horns, they'd grown outlandishly long.

ELK CHOPS WITH CUMBERLAND SAUCE

MIKE SCHOBY

ELK BACKSTRAPS are so good you have to be a bad chef and downright horrible human to turn them into an un-appetizing meal. Any way you cook an elk's backstrap, as long as you keep it medium to medium rare, will be damn tasty. This recipe takes an already great cut of meat to the next level.

THE MEAT

Cut backstraps across the grain into 1½- or 2-inch steaks. Dry rub, covering all surfaces, with Hi Mountain Steak Rub, and let stand in the fridge for a minimum of 30 minutes. Remove from fridge and let stand just before cooking.

While I have traditionally grilled these steaks over a bed of hardwood coals, I have recently been using a Camp Chef 14-inch cast iron skillet. Get the skillet screaming hot and put in a half stick of butter and two tablespoons of olive oil. Place the chops into the skillet on one side and tip the skillet about 20 degrees so the butter/oil pools on the opposite side from the steaks. With a spoon, baste the bubbling butter over the top of the chops. After approximately three minutes (or until the bottom is well seared), flip the chops and keep basting butter. The chops will be finished to medium rare in another three minutes. Remove from heat, cover in foil, and let them rest while you make the Cumberland sauce.

THE SAUCE

Pour excess butter out of the skillet (leave a tablespoon or so in the pan) and add ½ onion diced (sauté long enough to soften) followed by ½ cup of port wine, 1 cup of beef stock (elk stock if you have it), ½ teaspoon of dry mustard, ½ teaspoon of cayenne, ¼ cup of raspberry jelly, black pepper, and salt to taste. Slowly reduce until it thickens but is still pourable. I prefer the consistency of room temperature maple syrup. Put two steaks per plate and drizzle with the Cumberland sauce. Serve with a side of wild rice, a good artisan bread, and a bottle of Argentinian Malbec and you have a near-perfect meal. Don't gild the lily with this recipe; it doesn't need it.

Your friends will be talking about this meal for generations. It will become camp legend.

---

and wisely given up active pursuit and was cropping creek-bottom grasses like a lawnmower.

"You can shoot him if you want," Amos offered, too casually. I knew how he felt. Savvy and scarred, past his prime, the bull deserved some peace.

Although I'm never one to pass on the right animal, even at dawn on the first day, I'd been marinating in the richness of hunting a fantastic population of relatively undisturbed elk; watching bulls and cows perform their ancient dance. But the wind was changing. Snow was on its way, and as the fourth day dawned something was different. My appetite was pacified. I was well steeped in the experience, and it was time to find the right bull and shoot.

OPPORTUNITY KNOCKS

Although the day started slow, oppressed by lowering clouds and gusty winds, it quickened as we got deep into canyon bottoms and away from the wind. Wallows littered the canyonside we stalked down, reeking of the promise of fresh bull urine. It was quite clear that I had the right country, the right guide, and the right herd; now I just needed an opportunity.

Pinned by no less than eight bulls feeding on a grassy hillside across the bottom, we sat and glassed as the morning matured. Hot sun blared through the occasional break in the clouds, taking the humidity of last night's drizzle and churning it from refreshing to oppressive.

Midday beckoned. As we headed up the canyon, we bumped heads briefly with a bull that I probably would have shot but just didn't have time. The woods had quieted, and I stopped to strip layers, and then again just shy of a mountain meadow.

That's when Amos made a call and, as he gleefully put it later, "sucked that bull from half-a-mile up the ridge."

When the bull broke into view, he was galloping into the meadow, coming straight at us like a runaway racehorse, already well within range. Although his rack was narrow, the tines I could see were long and sweeping. I flicked the safety off.

A few previously unseen cows appeared to the left, and the bull stopped hard and bugled, facing me straight on perhaps 130 yards away. Unwilling to take the head-on shot, I sat still. From a distance, as through water, Amos whispered, "He's a nice bull."

Then that nice bull was gone, cutting through the aspens on the slope above. Scrambling to my feet, I watched, catching glimpses of dark legs walking steadily. Braced against the bole of an old quaky, I followed the bull in my scope, and as he passed through a narrow rift in the trees, I fired into his shoulder.

Still coming out of recoil, I worked the bolt fast as the bull swapped ends and lit out the way he'd come. I swung through his vitals and pressed off another shot, knowing as the rifle recoiled that I'd hit a tree. Then the bull was gone into a thick copse of pines.

Surfing waves of adrenaline, I scrambled up a slight bank and leaned against a tree, searching for movement. There was none.

After pausing to soak in the moment and still my jangling nerves, I approached the pines and found the bull just inside the edge, killed cleanly with the first shot.

After many, many photos, an informal autopsy showed that the InterBond had penetrated several inches of heavy shoulder muscle, smashed bone, scrambled both lungs, passed through the opposite ribs, and stopped against the hide in the crease behind the opposite shoulder. Classic lethal performance.

The fickle October sun retreated behind a curtain of clouds as we hauled the bull out, easing my fears that the meat would spoil in the heat. I babied the pre-'64 Super Grade Winchester, which had spoken with authority again after probably 30 years of silence in the shadows of a gun cabinet.

Sensory overload threatened. The best elk hunt of my life had just built to the perfect ending, punctuated with the perfect nostalgic rifle, bringing boyhood dreams to mature reality. ⑪

Modern Elk Caller's Handbook

Fool the most over-called, educated bulls in elk country with these new-age tactics.

Every veteran elk hunter worth his salt will agree: Calling in a bull today is a lot tougher than it was years ago.

In most areas, whether over-the-counter (OTC) public, private, or limited draw, elk are pressured. In some cases, wolves have caused them to alter habits and leave traditional rutting grounds. In many public areas, elk are over-called and educated. Hunters can't fashion a bugle out of a coiled copper tube, blow it aggressively, and expect bulls to come tromping in wild-eyed and blowing steam. The Golden Years of elk calling these are not.

To successfully call modern bulls, skill, understanding, and finesse are required.

While I've called my share of bulls, there are hunters who speak elk far more fluently than I do. So I tracked down two successful (if not legendary) elk callers to dig deeper into the tricks of the calling trade: Wayne Carlton, who needs no introduction, and Randsom Owens, an elk-talking freak who specializes in hunting monster trophy bulls in some of Utah's best limited-draw units.

To start with, it's not that elk are so educated that they are uncallable; you've just got to fluently speak the language—to spin the Primos phrase. Moreover, you've got to be aware of what I'll term "cultural nuances." To sell yourself as a non-intruder in elk society, you've got to be acutely aware of what makes them comfortable and uncomfortable. Owens, when attempting to call a bull in a highly pressured area, suggests you "bugle tentatively. Rake gently and thump the ground just a little. Don't thrash the tree you're raking; just brush it a bit . . . slowly."

On the other hand, when moving in on elk you've got to move and sound like elk. According to Owens, rutting bulls are very noisy, especially in the timber.

"If they hear soft sounds, really quiet sounds, they get suspicious," he said. "It doesn't hurt to make lots of noise when moving in on elk in the timber—breaking sticks, dragging your toe, or whatnot. Every once in a while, make a little cow call or grunt or a little raghorn call. But if you're making lots of aggressive bull sounds and being really quiet otherwise, those elk will get suspicious."

Use cow elk sounds far more than elk bugles. Be flexible and take the elk's temperature as you begin to call. Offer a bull security—which means comfortable, sociable cows.

"Crank a bull up slowly until he gets comfortable with what you're doing before you bugle," Carlton said. "Then do a high-pitched, aggravating bugle—not threatening, but aggravating, to make him come."

Don't attempt to predict what elk will do. Be willing to adapt.

"We need to remember that elk cannot read," Carlton advised. "They don't read the stories you and I read or the stories you and I write."

Elk don't know that they're supposed to be pressured, educated, horny, hungry, or anything else at a given time. They are what they are. As you begin working a herd or a bull, just listen, feel, and watch. Join the conversation as you get a feel for it and then don't dominate it. Be polite. Until you need to be that irritating young bull that needs a thrashing—or that seductive cow yearning for company.

A big mistake a lot of hunters make, in Owens's opinion, is that they don't know their local elk.

"Different populations make different sounds," he said. "Some sound a lot like the elk you commonly hear on TV, others make the most outlandish sounds you ever heard. I've brought in a lot of bulls without calling at all—just raking or just thumping. Really, it's an art form. When I'm observing elk, I pay attention to how a tree sounds when they rake it, how the ground sounds when they stomp. And at what point they step back from raking and stomp—things like that."

Get into elk country whenever possible, find elk, and listen. As Owens said, comfortable elk make some really bizarre sounds, and in high-pressure areas, callers adept at reproducing those sounds tend to be far more successful than hunters limited to stereotypical cow calls, calf mews, and bugles.

While reed-type calls are the easiest to master and thus appeal to neophyte callers, take the time to master diaphragm mouth calls. Diaphragm calls are more versatile than reed calls—with a little practice you can make sounds just as bizarre as the elk.

Diaphragm calls also have the sterling quality of being hands-free. That's particularly useful when bowhunting. As Carlton pointed out, "You don't want to have to put an elk call down to pick up whatever you need to be successful."

Also, you can make a high-pitched squeak on that call—even one that sounds kind of bad—and a departing bull will almost always turn broadside and hesitate for just a few seconds, long enough for you to send an arrow through his vitals.

Positioning before calling is also vital to success. Flank a rutting herd—always on the downwind side, as Owens pointed out—and move with them, waiting for the terrain to be favorable for you to set up and call. Very importantly,

according to Carlton, "Be where they want to be in the first place. Don't make it hard to get to you. For instance, during hot weather when most people don't want to be hunting, find cool shady places with water—elk want to be there, to wallow in it and drink it. Then call. Now you've got two things working for you."

Speaking of terrain, whether the land you hunt is public or private can have a huge bearing on how pressured the animals are—and thus on how you call. Although private land is often revered as the ultimate place to hunt elk, it might have as much or more pressure than public land. As Carlton pointed out, "On public, if you're willing to walk, you can hike away from the pressure. That's not the case on private land—you've got to hunt within the boundaries, where they may have been pressured. There might have been 40 hunters there before you."

Personally, that's been my experience with private-land elk hunts. When on a smallish (as elk country goes) piece of, say, 12,000 to 15,000 acres, you've got to hunt the elk like you'd hunt whitetails. Don't pressure them, or you'll never see them again. If you can't get on a bull, and you can't call him, back off and try again the next day. Frustrating, but it's better than running him miles away onto the neighbor's property.

Simple fact: Calling elk isn't as easy as it once was. That's plain. To be successful most of the time, you've just about got to have a doctorate in elk-speak and a master's degree in elk social studies. Neither can be researched or bought: Such knowledge must be earned the hard way, by time spent in elk country.

Luckily, there's no place a passionate elk hunter would rather be. So study the tips above and get into the woods to rub shoulders with a few elk. Ⓗ

CRAIG BODDINGTON

DIEHARD

THESE GAME ANIMALS ARE HARD TO KILL—DAMN HARD.

ARE SOME GAME animals "tougher" than others? Some veterinarians dispute this, and on some levels, they are correct. Dismantle the brain or sever the spinal cord and all game animals in the world are in trouble. Pierce the heart or its major vessels, or perforate both lungs, and the outcome is equally certain. On the other hand, based on long experience, I genuinely believe that some animals are hardier than others, perhaps possessed of greater vitality and will to survive...or perhaps just blessed with a slower nervous system. There are some animals that seem more impervious to "shock" than others and disregard absolutely mortal blows ... at least for a time. Here's my short list of really tough game animals, species that die hard and have earned my respect.

LEOPARD

The leopard is not a very big animal. A friend of mine, Dr. Ron Norman, took a monster back in 1979 that weighed in at 226 pounds. I have heard of a few more that legitimately weighed over 200 pounds, but this is extremely rare. A really big leopard might weigh 180 pounds, but as is the case with many animals, we like to exaggerate size. In most areas, mature, perfectly "shootable" toms will weigh in between 130 and 150 pounds. This is not a big animal.

So, then, why is it that so many leopards are wounded? Of all the dangerous game, the leopard is the most likely to get through all defenses and hurt you. This is because his small size and amazingly effective camouflage enables him to launch from close quarters...and his blinding speed makes him very difficult to stop. Because of this size, most leopard attacks are survivable.

However, in my experience not all wounded leopards will lie in wait to settle the score. In fact, in my time in Africa, as a hunter of a few leopards and an observer of many more leopard hunts, it seems to me that more leopards just keep going. When a leopard is wounded, the incidence of a lost animal seems to exceed those hair-raising charges.

The answer, of course, is shot placement. The leopard's vitals actually lie a bit farther

Photo Credit: Gary Kramer

back between the shoulders than with ungulates. This is greatly exaggerated when the leopard is reaching forward with its paws and feeding. Hence, the most common error is to shoot a bit too far forward. If you do there's going to be trouble. Likewise, if you hit too high, you may just shock the spine but not break it. Like with all animals, such a shot may knock the leopard out for a few seconds, but he'll quickly be up and gone.

In my experience, leopards shot too far forward or too high are very likely to be lost. While I certainly don't advocate shooting too far back, leopards hit a bit on the far side of the shoulder are often recovered, although they may wreak vengeance along the way. If a leopard is standing broadside, a shoulder shot one-third up into the body is certain, but in poor light, or if the leopard is reaching forward to feed, it is safer and much more certain to consciously aim just behind the shoulder, again one-third to no more than one-half up into the body.

A leopard's body is built for all sorts of athletic activities. Its long, slender frame is all muscle, and its sharp, foldable claws can do some real damage in close quarters.

There's one more thing. The majority of leopards I have seen lost have been shot with .375s. This is counter-intuitive until you really think about it. The .375 and the majority of its bullets were designed for animals several times the size of a leopard. Large-caliber bullets designed to penetrate will do exactly that, and they will essentially punch through on a leopard without doing much damage.

Since the leopard is "dangerous game," some countries require a minimum caliber, and if that's the case, obviously follow the law. Given a choice, however, I am convinced that a "deer caliber" with a fairly quick-expanding "deer bullet" will anchor a leopard much more quickly. Because while he isn't big, this dangerous cat must not be underestimated.

DIE HARD

The wolf's anatomy just screams tough. Their powerful bodies are equipped with a heavily muscled neck for power and long legs that allow them to move easily over rocky terrain and deep snow.

WOLF

The wolf has generally been hunted as an "add-on," taken as a target of opportunity when encountered on hunts in Canada and Alaska (and, for that matter, on many mountain hunts in Asia). This is changing. Specific "winter wolf hunts" are becoming more popular in the Far North, and with wolf season now reopened in several states, a lot of tags are being sold and more hunters are specifically trying for a wolf.

However, provided one considers the wolf a big-game animal—which I surely do—there is no animal in North America as elusive as a wolf, especially when hunted on purpose rather than taken by accident.

Actually, far more wolves are taken by trapping than by hunting, so relatively few hunters have much experience shooting them. But many of us have lots of experience shooting coyotes. I think everyone would agree that coyotes are extremely tough; pound for pound as

Boddington shot this wolf, a third in a set of three killed on one stand. A .300 magnum took down this dog. Even with this big caliber, his will to survive was astonishing.

tough as any animal I have hunted. This applies to all canines. And the wolf is, at minimum, twice the size of any coyote. Larger males can be up to four times larger.

Not only that, but wolves are used to surviving harsh winters and constant fighting for dominance...or just to survive as part of the pack. The biggest wolf is no larger than a medium-sized deer—very few will exceed 150 pounds —but in my experience (some good, some not so good) the wolf has far greater vitality and will to live than any ungulate.

If you hit a wolf well, in the chest cavity, with an expanding bullet, you will surely get him...but even with a devastating hit you may have to do a bit more tracking than you expect. In snow this is not so difficult, but on bare ground it can be very hard. Serious Northern wolf hunters often use relatively small rifles—semi-automatic .223s are favorites—but they do

most of their wolf hunting in snow and wish to minimize pelt damage.

It's no secret that I have had my difficulties with wolves, so in the last few years I've carried mostly fast big-game calibers with bullets designed to expand. With this formula I've taken five wolves (not all in North America). Three, hit perfectly, were down on the spot. Another, also hit perfectly, traveled 200 yards. The last, hit not quite so perfectly, took a going-away shot from a .300 Weatherby Magnum with a 180-grain bullet. We found it dead, but we trailed it nearly a half-mile into thick timber. To me the wolf is not only one of our most elusive animals, but also a truly great game animal and matchless trophy. He's pound for pound one of the toughest. Hit him well, but also hit him plenty hard. The chances for a shot are slim enough that you don't want to blow your one-and-only opportunity.

A bear's body is built for strength, not neccesaily speed. Short, muscle-laden legs, massive shoulders, and a short back make for a compact package that's hard to take down.

BIG BEARS

Big bears are just plain tough, and the bigger they are, the harder they fall. This applies to all bears pretty much equally. A really big black bear can be bigger than an average interior grizzly. Such a bear is an altogether different creature from the average 200-pound black bear—but even small and medium-sized bears are tough; it's just a matter of degree and magnitude as bears get bigger.

Although highly intelligent creatures, bears have relatively slow nervous systems that seem impervious to shock. (After all, in winter they sleep for months on end.) It isn't unusual to see a bear drop to a shot, apparently stone dead...and then get right back up as if nothing had happened. At close range bears may immediately charge upon receiving a bullet, perhaps more frequently than wolves, leopards, or buffalo. More likely, however, a stricken bear will head for thick cover with all the strength that remains. He'll wait for you there.

These things can be true of a mid-sized black bear. They are just as true—and a lot more frightening—with an Alaskan giant weighing possibly 1,500 pounds. Because of the strength, tenacity, and ferocity when wounded, bears should only be taken with relatively close and certain shots, and shot placement is essential. Most experienced bear hunters and bear guides are adamant about shoulder shots, aiming for the chest so as to take out at least one shoulder. Well-constructed bullets designed to penetrate are essential, and the caliber must be adequate. I figure the .338 Winchester Magnum to be the sensible minimum for use on big bears.

Cape buffalo are equipped with the toughest build on this list. Their massive shoulders, stocky legs, large head, and heavy-set frame are just simply hard to stop.

CAPE BUFFALO

Even though they're often referred to as "black death" and other scary nicknames, difficulties with unwounded African buffalo are very rare. In thick cover there's always the chance of blundering into a buffalo within its "fight rather than flight" radius, and while working a herd it's unwise to get between a cow and her calf, but in general simply hunting a buffalo isn't a particularly dangerous undertaking...until that first shot is fired. If the caliber and bullet are adequate and the shot is directed properly, that's pretty

© michael.luckett-fotolia.com

much the end of the story—lots of tension but little drama.

Ah, but place that first shot poorly and the game changes quickly! I don't know if African buffalo have overdeveloped adrenal glands, a hyped-up nervous system from dealing with lions all their lives, or if they're just plain tough. Whatever the case, the Cape buffalo is very strong and powerful, and if the first shot doesn't do the trick, it might take a bunch more to get the job done. One of

Jack O'Connor's more famous stories was about a buffalo in Tanganyika that required 14 large-caliber hits before succumbing. I have never seen one take quite that much, but genuine, pure one-shot kills are fairly rare—even if the first shot is extremely well-placed.

Here's the deal: Upon receiving a bullet a buffalo usually doesn't turn and charge. Instead, he usually turns the other way and heads for cover. The legend is that he will then circle on his trail and lay an

ambush for his tormentors. Yes, some will...but many will simply keep going as long as they are able. The most likely outcome when a buffalo is hit poorly is not a hair-raising charge, but that the buffalo will never be seen again. Sometimes, in thick cover or especially in herds, there is simply no chance for a follow-up shot. But all too often, hunters place that first shot as well as they can... and then wait to see what happens next. No matter how good it looked, until you recover the animal you won't know how perfect that first shot really was, and even if placement was perfect, you have no idea how well the bullet actually performed.

Though body-shot buffalo rarely drop in their tracks, I've seen many

This Zimbabwe buffalo was taken with a fairly rare one-shot kill with a standard shoulder shot. The only reason this happened was because Boddington was using a single shot and the bull got into the herd before another shot could be fired.

African plains game comes in all shapes and sizes. Big bodies and small, thick hides and thick skin are among the group. One thing they all have in common: the will to live.

drop within 50 yards to shoulder or lung shots. On the other hand, I've seen several that went a quarter mile or more after receiving seemingly fatal chest shots. Some were still standing, ready to fight. In open country I've seen buffalo taken down very cleanly with good bullets from light calibers, but the general legal minimum of 9.3mm (.366) or .375 caliber makes sense, preferably with a good, tough expanding bullet for the first shot, followed up by solid(s) when the buffalo turns away and makes for cover. Buffalo are herd animals, and when things are happening fast, they look pretty much alike, so follow-up shots cannot be fired unless you're certain you're on the same buff. But if you're sure, then I believe follow-up shots should be fired so long as the buffalo remains on its feet. Your buffalo hunt hasn't really been dangerous yet...but it gets deadly when you take up the blood trail.

AFRICAN PLAINS GAME

African game is legendary for its toughness. To some extent this is a myth, but behind most legends and myths there is a grain of truth. Africa's prey species develop in a predator-rich environment. In wild Africa they still have to dodge cats and canines great and small on a daily basis. Because of this, I believe that African game is generally edgier, more keyed up, than many species with which we are more familiar. It is true that most African antelope, even the very small ones, can take a solid hit through both lungs and travel farther than one might expect. And don't even think about how far the trail might lead if you hit too far back. We Americans tend to prefer that double-lung shot because it offers the largest target and spoils the least amount of edible meat, but African professional hunters generally recommend the shoulder shot, through the heart or just over the top of the heart, because it absolutely works more quickly.

That said, I don't believe all African animals are equal in toughness when hit in the shoulder. Here's a short list of the toughness of the plains variety.

ELAND

The eland is the largest of all antelope, with a big bull of the Livingstone or Central African giant eland races weighing as much as a solid ton. This is bigger than any buffalo, and because of sheer size, caliber and bullet selection are important. But the eland is not tough for his size and succumbs readily to a well-placed bullet. Many who hunt them will be surprised, though, at how elusive this big antelope really can be in the open plains of Africa.

BUSHBUCK

Lest it appear that I'm picking on the spiral-horned tribe, the bushbuck, the smallest of this group, is very tough for his size. Also, he is among few antelope

IMPALA

Another small antelope that is notoriously hardy (though not aggressive) is the impala, maybe 140 pounds of great venison but seemingly immune to bullet shock. As former partner Tim Danklef once said, "If impala were as big as buffalo, we'd all be dead."

ZEBRA

Lest we overlook Africa's many prey species that are not antelope, we arrive at the zebra. Never underestimate a zebra. A big stallion might weigh 800 pounds and is very, very strong. Poorly hit zebra may be tracked endlessly and are often not recovered. Obviously, the sure cures for such problems are: Use enough gun, use enough bullet, and be careful with your shot. ⑪

with a reputation for ferocity when cornered. Few races weigh more than 125 pounds...but you'd better hit a bushbuck properly.

NYALA

Ethiopia's unique mountain nyala, genetically closer to the bushbuck than kudu or nyala, is also very tough. I've hunted them twice, no problems, but among the relatively few hunters I know who have pursued this magnificent antelope, I know a full half-dozen who have wounded and lost their mountain nyala. Ouch.

THE APEX CHALLENGE

A LIFELONG CHASE FOR NORTH AMERICA'S APEX PREDATOR ENDS IN THE BARREN LANDSCAPE OF THE FROZEN ALBERTA TUNDRA.

CRAIG BODDINGTON

IT WAS A balmy 26 below zero, sort of the way things are in Northern Canada in January. Honestly, the thermometer didn't mean so much because it was dead calm. This was good, but since I hate cold weather, it was not especially comfortable. But, this was my idea, and my fast-freezing toes were paying the price. As it happened, there wasn't as much to worry about as I might have expected. I'd only been there a couple hours when I saw dog-like forms at the bend in the river to my right.

Almost exactly a year earlier videographer Mike Emery and I had sat on the same bluff, overlooking the same frozen river, watching old tracks on the ice, sitting and shivering for over nine hours and more, hoping wolves would return to the enticing bait we were watching. They did—in the night—but not when we needed them to be there. But that's part of wolf hunting. You are likely to put in a lot of time without seeing a wolf. Honestly, on any given day I have no idea what the odds might be, but they are low.

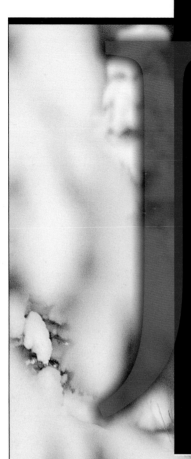

CHANCE ENCOUNTERS

J ust a year earlier, north of Cambridge Bay on Canada's Victoria Island, we were hunting caribou when we jumped two grey wolves. It was a classic chance encounter, and the shot would have been easy, but it wasn't legal for me to take a wolf, so we watched them run over the next ridge. Wolves are well distributed in northern Canada and Alaska —up there they are not and never have been endangered or threatened— but they are wary and elusive, and sightings are not common. I have wanted to take a North American wolf for a long time, so I can recall with some clarity each time I've seen one. Collectively, I've seen quite a few, but seeing a wolf and taking home its pelt are not the same thing.

Last May, my wife, Donna, and I were on a bear hunt in Southeast Alaska. We had taken our bears and were lounging in "camp"—actually a very comfortable boat—when we spotted a wolf trotting along the shoreline. We jumped in a skiff and tried to get ahead of him, but he vanished into the forest before we could get there. I figure we missed him by less than a minute. Which is pretty much the story of my life, at least when it comes to wolves.

I FIRST HUNTED in "wolf country" in 1973. That's in quotes because my definition of wolf country is not just a place where wolves live, but also where wolves can be hunted. With grey wolves now delisted (meaning officially no longer considered endangered) in the United States wolf country has expanded considerably. I actually saw a wolf in western Montana while hunting elk in November 2012, my first sighting in the Lower 48, but I can't count that as a lost opportunity because I didn't have a wolf tag.

However, since 1973 I have purchased a boatload of wolf tags. In those 41 years I haven't sojourned into wolf country every single year, but I certainly have a number of times. Although wolves are shy and are not often seen, they are very much a part of the northern wilderness. So when in wolf country with wolf season open, one always carries a wolf tag, and in the fullness of time, most experienced northern hunters eventually take a wolf. Lee Hoots, former editor of this publication, took a black wolf on his very first Canadian hunt. Another buddy, Dwight Van Brunt, shot a gorgeous dark wolf on a Dall sheep hunt in the Arctic. Note that dastardly characters like these couldn't be satisfied with just shooting wolves, they had to rub it in by shooting the color phase that wolf hunters drool over.

OPPORTUNITIES WON AND LOST

It appears that biologists have now decided to call our northern wolf *Canis lupus*, the "grey wolf." This does differentiate the northern wolf from the smaller Mexican red wolf, which remains legitimately endangered, but the animal we call "timber wolf" or "grey wolf" doesn't live just in timber and certainly isn't always grey. The most common color is probably tan with black or grey highlights, but colors vary from pure white to pure black and everything in between. Me, I always wanted a black wolf, but nobody hunts wolves specifically for color.

From what I have seen, I think the moose-killing wolves of Canada and Alaska are probably the largest, but I don't think there is significant biological difference between our wolves and wolves of Eurasia. Chance encounters happen there, too, and under many circumstances, the North American ritual of purchasing a license or tag doesn't apply. The season is open or it is not. In 2005 I shot a wolf in Mongolia, and in 2003 I missed one in Tajikistan.

Probably the best wolf hunting in the world is in Macedonia, a very small country plagued by about 2,500 sheep-eating wolves. The local hunters do driven hunts for wild boar and wolf, and hunting over bait is amazingly reliable. I got a nice wolf over bait there in 2010 with little difficulty, but wolf depredation on livestock is a serious issue, and hunting is the primary means for keeping the population in check. The difference is that, in the European fashion, hunting is allowed at night, which really changes the game.

We can't do that in North America, so the odds are considerably decreased... but I have had opportunities. Years ago, I was sitting on a black bear bait in northern Canada, and instead of the big bear I was expecting, a huge wolf appeared on top of the bait pile. At the shot he turned inside out and vanished behind the bait. Ⓗ

I THOUGHT MY EYES WERE PLAYING TRICKS ON ME WHEN THE WOLVES APPEARED

I THOUGHT I had him, so I waited a couple of minutes, collecting myself, and then went forward to claim my prize. No wolf, no blood, no hair, no tracks... nothing. It spooked me so bad that I had a passing thought that I'd imagined the whole thing. So I went back to the blind and found my empty cartridge case. It smelled of freshly burnt powder, so I apparently had shot at something. I probably shot right over him, and what I took to be the wolf taking the bullet was probably said wolf making a very fast exit.

Another time, in Alaska, we were camped on one side of a river, and a wolf came loping along the far bank. I grabbed my rifle and rolled him with a really brilliant running shot, but he recovered and vanished into some thick willows. It took a while to get across the river, but this time there was good blood and what appeared to be shoulder bone. So far, so good. Then it started to rain buckets. All sign was instantly wiped away, and although we spent the day searching desperately, we never found another trace.

TRYING AGAIN

Over the years there were other long-range sightings of wolves, and lots more unfilled wolf tags, but that explains how I got to 2013 in a wolf-less state...and also, having been beaten badly, why I wanted one so desperately. "Obsessed" is too strong a word, but I really wanted a wolf, at least in part to clear my record. Like all hunters, I have missed and messed up now and again, but our grey wolf is the only animal

I can think of that I hadn't taken because of some personal folly.

I met Alberta outfitter Trent Packham (groatcreekoutfitters.com) at a Safari Club fundraiser in Michigan. An avid trapper as well as hunter, I liked him, and he seemed to know his wolves. Alberta is not as well-known for winter wolf hunting, but Trent's country near Whitecourt, northwest of Edmonton, has a lot of moose, a lot of deer, and quite a few elk preyed upon by wolves (along with cougars, coyotes, and bears). Perhaps uniquely, Alberta treats wolves much the same as coyotes—inexpensive license, no tags, and no bag limit. Predation on game and depredation on livestock is considered a serious issue. Trappers adhere to different and complex rules, but sport hunting for wolves, though encouraged, is not considered an effective means of controlling wolf populations.

I set up a hunt for the end of January 2013 and everything seemed perfect—except the weather warmed up to a freakishly unseasonal 40 degrees, and all wolf movement went nocturnal. On the last day it turned cold again. We got into a pack and almost howled one up, and Trent and I both believed we needed just another day or two. But that isn't always possible, so we agreed to try again in January 2014.

GETTING IT DONE

So here I was on the bluff above a frozen river, definitely my favorite spot from the year before. It was obviously a good traveling corridor, and there were lots of

wolf tracks of various vintages. Trent receives road-killed moose from the local highway department, so the situation was sweetened by a moose carcass on the ice, much chewed by birds and various predators.

I was in a ground blind tucked against a stout spruce, relatively comfortable—especially after I put on the insulated body suit Trent had left with me. (Hey, when it's cold, I'm a sniveling wimp.) I used the long Arctic twilight before sunrise to figure things out. My rangefinder said the bait was almost precisely 200 yards away, but 100 yards almost straight down. I'd need to be very careful to hold in the bottom third, lest I slip over the top. I set up my favorite African Sporting Creations shooting sticks, and I realized because of the steep angle I'd need to get the rifle barrel well outside the mesh window. Trent had specifically authorized me to either shoot through the screen or cut it. I opened my knife, practiced the motion to cut the mesh, and stuck it in the packed snow at my feet. I checked the Blaser once more, chamber loaded, uncocked. Then, chemical hand warmers in my gloves, I grabbed a Nelson DeMille novel and settled in for what I expected to be a very long and very cold day.

I thought my eyes were playing tricks on me when the wolves appeared just like they were supposed to, but also like I had come to believe they never would. I waited until they were opposite the blind, approaching the bait, and then I did the drill I'd practiced: Grab the knife, cut the mesh, drop the knife, reach slowly for the

A look down from the author's vantage point on a bluff high above the frozen river shows the first two wolves lying dead on the ice.

rifle, set it gently over the sticks and slide the barrel out. The sun was coming up over the ridge on the far side of the river, in my face, but the wolves were in deep shadow, not easy to see. I was convinced the first wolf was the largest, but there was no definition of color. I didn't even know he was dark, let alone black. I held low on the chest, fired, heard the bullet thunk home and hesitated a half-second. The wolf was down.

The other two were already starting to run, and I was now operating on pure reflex. The straight-pull Blaser was already reloaded, and I swung past the second animal, heard that bullet hit and saw the wolf go down cleanly. By now, the third wolf was at 250 yards and gaining ground fast, but going nearly straight away. I gave it a slight lead and was astonished to hear that bullet hit as well and even more surprised to see that wolf drop in a heap. Here's where I made my first mistake: I swung back to check the first two, belatedly realized I needed to reload, and when I looked back the third wolf was back up and nearly in the timber at the

bend of the river. I tried to hit it again and failed. Then my hands started to shake.

The first wolf was coal black, a huge male, probably the alpha of the pack. And yes, it was a pack...a group Trent had seen and believed to number 14. The rest of the pack, certainly including subadults, hadn't yet come out of the timber when I fired,

and they immediately started howling, looking for their leader. The second was dark charcoal gray, almost black. We found the third dead inside the timber, also a big wolf, brown and tan with gray highlights. We took pictures with wolves howling on the ridge above us, a morning well worth a 40-year wait. Ⓗ

5 PLACES to FIND BIG BEARS NOW

CRAIG BODDINGTON

FROM NORTH TO SOUTH
& COAST TO COAST,

HERE'S WHERE TO FIND
BIG BEARS THIS SPRING.

EXACTLY WHY is a mystery even to me, but I get an extra-special thrill out of bear hunting. This is a problem, because I can't really justify hunting another brown or grizzly bear. Black bears are easier. Though not as mean and nasty as most lawyers, they're just as plentiful, a lot better looking, and I presume, a lot tastier. Handled right, black bear meat is actually pretty good, and hunting them offers just the hint of genuine danger. So, if I were to start planning a black bear hunt, where might I look? Wow, that's a wide-open field. Now that a few black bears have taken up residence in extreme southeastern Kansas, black bears actually occur in all of the Lower 48 States, plus Alaska, and in all the Canadian provinces. For that matter, they also occur throughout northern Mexico, although numbers are still building and hunting opportunities are few. So, throughout that vast range, exactly where would I plan a bear hunt?

Well, if I lived in bear country, I'd strongly consider hunting my own backyard. However, I'd also take a hard look at where I live, who I know and what I know. No one in the U.S. or Canada all that far from good black bear hun Though not as numerous as white they now number into the mil and actually occupy a larger range the whitetail. But do you have the and the know-how (or local contac

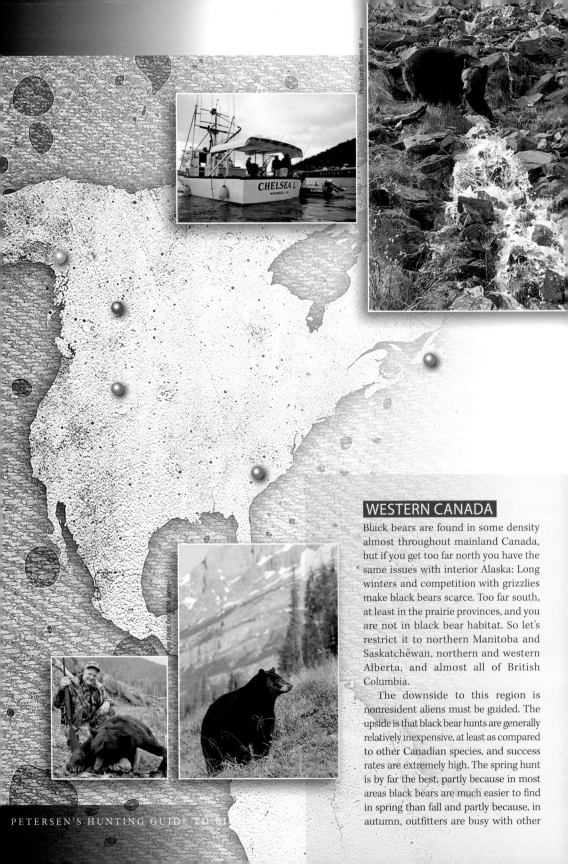

Photo Credit: Donald M. Jones

CHELSEA L

Photo Credit: Donald M. Jones

WESTERN CANADA

Black bears are found in some density almost throughout mainland Canada, but if you get too far north you have the same issues with interior Alaska: Long winters and competition with grizzlies make black bears scarce. Too far south, at least in the prairie provinces, and you are not in black bear habitat. So let's restrict it to northern Manitoba and Saskatchewan, northern and western Alberta, and almost all of British Columbia.

The downside to this region is nonresident aliens must be guided. The upside is that black bear hunts are generally relatively inexpensive, at least as compared to other Canadian species, and success rates are extremely high. The spring hunt is by far the best, partly because in most areas black bears are much easier to find in spring than fall and partly because, in autumn, outfitters are busy with other

SOUTHEAST ALASKA

Black bears are well distributed across interior Alaska, but because of harsh conditions and an inability to compete with brown/grizzly bears, their population is pretty thin. In most of Alaska there's nothing wrong with having a black bear tag in your pocket while hunting other game, but actual sightings are uncommon. The big exception is southeast Alaska, where black bears are plentiful.

Black bear hunting in Alaska is extremely democratic. Most guide/outfitters in good country do black bear hunts, but many also offer the unique opportunity of combining black bear with brown bear. This is also an Alaskan "do-it-yourself" hunt that makes a lot of sense. In Alaskan lexicon, there are licensed guides...but there are also "outfitters" and "transporters" who cannot legally guide, but can take you to a good hunting area.

I have hunted black bear in southeast Alaska several ways: guided and unguided; on foot by backpack; and by boat. While I have not always been successful on other species, I have actually never failed to take a black bear when I had an Alaskan tag!

Black bear hunting is open both fall and spring, but my spin on the best time and the best way is in the spring, by boat. I've done this both guided and unguided: using a licensed guide whose base camp is a boat and using a transporter with a boat. In Alaska a transporter cannot make decisions regarding the hunt and cannot touch game, but the boat sure does make a nice camp! An alternative to these options is simply renting a boat for a week, which is possible in many southeast Alaska communities.

In much of southeast Alaska the conifer jungle just off the beach is so thick as to be impenetrable, so you're really hunting a narrow shoreline. That's where the boat comes into play. In the spring bears are beachcombers, munching sedge grass to get their systems going and looking for carrion. You actually glass from the boat, covering ground. In a small boat you must make camp on shore; in a larger boat you "camp" on board, cruising and glassing in the late afternoon and running ashore in a smaller skiff, either when a bear is spotted or to hunt some likely coves. Either way, you can fish or put out crab pots and feast your way to your bear!

HUNTER:
DAVID HONEYCUTT JR.

STATE:
NORTH CAROLINA

BEAR WEIGHT:
784 LBS.

Some hunters spend their lives chasing a trophy-class bear. David Honeycutt spent about 30 minutes. The 16-year-old Wilmington, North Carolina, resident and a friend were sent out to search for tracks early in the morning on a 7,500-acre farm in Hyde County. They quickly found a fresh set and returned to the farmhouse. Hounds and hunters convened at the tracks. The dogs struck almost immediately. It took even less time to bay the bear in the thick Carolina pines. Honeycutt carried a borrowed lever-action .45-70, a rifle he never even fired before. As he and the dog handler approached the frantic hounds, the bear broke and passed within yards. Honeycutt raised his rifle, squeezed the trigger and found his mark. The 784-pound bear, the second-largest taken in NC, was dead within seconds.

species. In the spring they can concentrate on bear hunting.

In the heavy forests of northern Manitoba and Saskatchewan, most black bear hunting is done over bait. Alberta is a mix, depending on the area; some hunting is done over bait, while in other areas spot-and-stalk hunting is the rule. Baiting is not done in British Columbia, so black bears are hunted by glassing and stalking. Given a choice, I prefer glassing and stalking to sitting over bait, but that's a personal preference; which is better depends on the country and vegetation. In order to effectively glass for bears, you simply must have vantage points and enough open areas to see bears moving. So, in unbroken forest, baiting is essential; in hills or mountains you can glass.

I've neither taken a bear nor purchased a bear license in Saskatchewan, but over the years, I've hunted multiple times in

Alberta, British Columbia, and Manitoba. Most of these areas are "two-bear" areas. I haven't always taken two bears, but I can honestly say I have never had an unsuccessful spring black bear hunt in these three provinces. In Alaska, the eastern seaboard, and Vancouver Island, most black bears are black. In the western mainland, both in Canada and the United States, "color phase" bears are relatively common. A large percentage will almost always be black, but a fair number of bears are some shade of brown—from blonde to cinnamon to chocolate. You can hunt black bears for size or for color...my experience is that lighter-colored bears usually aren't big or old, and research suggests that lighter bears may grow darker as they get older. Western Canada offers a great opportunity for taking a brown black bear, and since two bears are usually allowed, you can hunt for both size and color.

NORTH CAROLINA

This one is a sleeper. Black bears are well distributed in all the Appalachian states, but northeastern North Carolina is a genuine hotspot for big black bears. Hyde County, adjoining both the coast and the huge Lake Mattamuskeet, is probably the center. There is a drawback: The season is only in the fall, which in my experience is not the best time for black bear movement. There is also a bonus: Hound hunting is legal (by county), which very much overcomes this obstacle.

Technically, this could be a very good do-it-yourself area. There are adequate public lands, plenty of bears, and big bears. Realistically though, unless you know someone, the best opportunity is with a local houndsman.

I've taken a number of nice bears, and in almost every imaginable color phase, but in 40 years I've taken just three "really big" black bears. The biggest was in the Kootenay region of British Columbia in 1974. I wish I still had it, but it was big

enough that the taxidermist stole the skull, and the rug went in a burglary 15 years later. Next biggest was on a friend's place near Lake Mattamuskeet in North Carolina. I was in a high stand, as if for whitetail, and the bear came out of a cornfield shortly after daylight. Although it weighed nearly 500 pounds, I'm not at all sure I did the right thing...while I was there two larger bears were taken! The last was on a do-it-yourself Alaska hunt the following year.

NEWFOUNDLAND

Okay, I'll admit it: I have never taken a black bear in Newfoundland. But I have never been on a "dedicated" black bear hunt in Newfoundland, and I have never hunted the spring bear season there. In the Northeast black bear hunting is traditional in Maine, Vermont, and New Hampshire. It has recently opened in New Jersey. Pennsylvania is famous for producing some monster bears, and the mountains of western New York hold a good population.

All of northeastern Canada is also good, but in this region, I think Newfoundland is the place to go. The "Newfie" black bear is actually a recognized sub-species: *Ursus americanus hamiltoni*. These bears are black, almost no color phase bears, but they are somewhat larger than mainland bears, right at 300 pounds average, a very good average weight. Absent wolves, cougars, and grizzlies, the black bear is the alpha predator in Newfoundland, and the primary cause of mortality of moose calves—in a place that has the most dense moose population in North America. So "Newfie" bears are well fed, they grow

large, and in the spring they come readily to bait.

That I haven't taken a black bear in Newfoundland is altogether my fault. I have hunted there five times, always in the fall, always for moose and/or caribou, and always with a black bear tag in my pocket. In the course of those trips, I always saw bear sign and usually glassed one or two bears—but I was looking for moose or caribou, so I never actually stalked any of the bears I saw.

Even though I've seen several nice bears, I would not hunt Newfoundland for black bear in the fall. Like most areas in Canada, a licensed guide is required, and few even offer a specialized fall black bear hunt, but many Newfoundland outfitters offer dedicated spring bear hunts. Baiting is allowed, and success is high. If I lived east of the Mississippi, this is a black bear hunt I would consider, based both on success and potential size of bears. For those who live in the region, you can actually "drive" to the island province of Newfoundland by using a ferry—a fun trip and a good way to go.

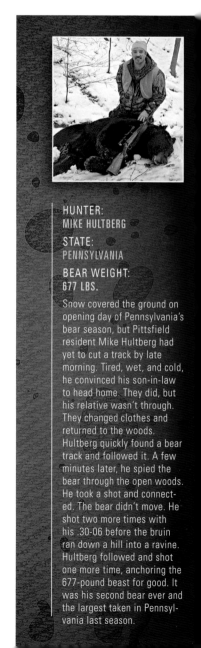

HUNTER:
MIKE HULTBERG

STATE:
PENNSYLVANIA

BEAR WEIGHT:
677 LBS.

Snow covered the ground on opening day of Pennsylvania's bear season, but Pittsfield resident Mike Hultberg had yet to cut a track by late morning. Tired, wet, and cold, he convinced his son-in-law to head home. They did, but his relative wasn't through. They changed clothes and returned to the woods. Hultberg quickly found a bear track and followed it. A few minutes later, he spied the bear through the open woods. He took a shot and connected. The bear didn't move. He shot two more times with his .30-06 before the bruin ran down a hill into a ravine. Hultberg followed and shot one more time, anchoring the 677-pound beast for good. It was his second bear ever and the largest taken in Pennsylvania last season.

Photo Credit: Donald M. Jones

MONTANA

I took my first black bear in the Bitterroot Mountains of southwestern Montana back in 1973. My next black bear hunt will be an unguided hunt in northwestern Montana, the first week of June 2015. Black bear hunting is very good throughout most of the Western states, but Montana gets my nod because bear hunting is still done in both spring and fall and Montana has 30 million acres of public land, much of it occupied by black bears. So opportunities are virtually unlimited for both guided and unguided hunting. In Montana black bear hunting is by spot-and-stalk. Neither baiting nor hounds are allowed.

Western Montana is almost certainly the right area, with lots of mountains, lots of bears, and lots of public land. Depending on area, the fall season runs in early September for archery, and then September 15 to November 30 for rifle. But if you're serious about a bear, go in the spring. I've already mentioned that, for spot-and-stalk hunting, you need country conducive to glassing. Montana has plenty of that, but one more thing is needed: bears moving where they can be seen! Fresh out of hibernation and hungry, bears are simply more active in the spring. I've hunted the West for 50 years, and I've seen just a handful of bears in the fall. Montana's spring bear season, depending on area, runs from April 15 to June 15. What is best depends altogether on when the bears come out of hibernation, and that varies depending on the harshness and length of winter. April is generally too early and May is fine, but in northern Montana early June is awesome. Ⓗ

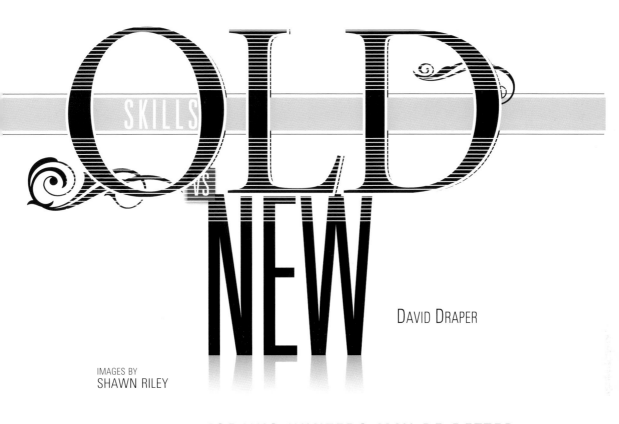

OLD SKILLS VS NEW

David Draper

IMAGES BY
SHAWN RILEY

TODAY'S HUNTERS MAY BE BETTER EQUIPPED WITH HIGH-TECH GEAR... BUT HAVE THEY LOST THEIR SKILLS?

IN A WORLD where boys can no longer be boys and pointing a finger on the playground gets a kid kicked out of school, it's hard to argue with old-timers who say we're raising a generation of wimps. Even in the woods, it's easy to believe we've lost our edge when gadgets have trumped experience. But were the good old days really so good? We're tagging more and bigger deer than ever before, and we're doing it in less time in the woods. Ah, there's the crux—modern man has become a better killer, but are we really better hunters? Let's take a look at seven essential skills and see who's really doing it better.

ORIENTEERING

MAP & COMPASS VS GPS

With a quick glance at his topographic map, the hunter schooled in traditional orienteering sees not just squiggly lines on paper, but mountain peaks, deep canyons, and wide saddles where he's likely to find elk. He understands scale and minutes and how close the contour lines lay tells him he must be ready to climb steep grades or navigate around sheer cliffs. His compass? A literal arrow pointing the way into and out of the woods safely. He knows how to take a bearing off a distant landmark and make his way to it, no matter what kind of country lays between him and his destination.

It's a modern miracle that connects the GPS-equipped hunter with dozens of satellites orbitting the earth. An LED indicator in the palm of his hand flashes his exact location and delivers a spreadsheet of information, from elevation to estimated time of arrival to marked waypoints. These waypoints allow the modern hunter to mark stand sites and animal sign and return to those exact spots many years later. Downloadable maps show boundary lines and landowner information, keeping him legal at all times and showing him hidden easements to landlocked hunting areas.

PERSPECTIVE

To paraphrase Daniel Boone, the traditional hunter may never have been lost, but he may have gotten confused for a few days at a time. In whiteout conditions or under the cover of darkness, navigating via map and compass is difficult for all but the most skilled woodsman. On the flipside, batteries die, technology fails, and, even with modern equipment, satellites can be hard to lock onto, especially in dark timber and deep canyons. Instead, the savvy hunter keeps a compass close at hand, a map in his hip pocket, and a GPS in his pack.

SCOUTING

READING SIGN VS TRAIL CAMERAS

From the moment he steps into the field, the traditional woodsman is on full alert. He sees not just the obvious signs, but also subtle changes in the scenery. A tuft of hair and a few disturbed leaves tell him where a wise, old buck left the trail to bed down. He looks closely at the landscape and tests the wind with his nose, finding a hidden wallow ripe with fresh elk sign. Like the native hunters before him, the grizzled vet is just as apt to sit quietly as he is to stalk through the timber, waiting for what little ripples of disturbance he has caused to settle and the woods to accept his presence.

Well before season, today's hunter has his trail cameras in place. From the comfort of his computer, the hunter watches bucks grow antlers and shed velvet, naming each one and knowing its habits. The modern hunter often picks a singular deer to hunt and focuses his scouting strategy on that buck alone. Through the use of multiple cameras, the hunter learns its patterns and establishes prime stand sites, so on opener he's waiting for the moment when, like clockwork, the buck he now considers "his" steps into the shooting lane, putting a quick end to a long-season of electronic scouting.

PERSPECTIVE

For the modern hunter, the kill can be almost anticlimactic. With his laser-focus on a singular animal, he's also missing everything the woods has to offer, which often includes bigger trophies smart enough to avoid the paparazzi of trail cameras. The traditional hunter, on the other hand, revels in the beauty of the outdoors, but may go home empty-handed. Judicious use of trail cameras, along with a deeper understanding of woodsmanship, not only can increase success rates, but also can lead to a greater enjoyment of the actual act of hunting.

DRESSING

NATURAL FIBERS

VS

Natty Bumppo was nicknamed Leather-stocking for a reason. He wore deerskin britches made from a buck he killed himself. And while leather may have gone out of favor for everyone except aging rockstars, many other natural materials are still worn by hunters today. Whether he admits it or not, the hunter who goes afield in oilskin is making a fashion statement, just saying no to less-durable nylon materials. Same goes for woolens, though newer materials and manufacturing techniques have taken away the itch and made the insulating fibers soft against the skin. Down, too, has gotten an upgrade with waterproof treatments, meaning a rainstorm is no longer a death knell for those wearing feathers.

MODERN MATERIALS

Wearing materials plucked from the Final Frontier—and we don't mean Alaska—the space-age hunter has technology on his side. Modern materials are able at once to be completely waterproof, yet still breathable, so hunters stay comfortable on long, hot hikes in the rain and snow. Moisture-wicking materials keep skin dry, while synthetic insulations are lighter and warmer than they've ever been. Hardware, too, has gotten an upgrade, with zippers that are waterproof and snaps that are silent so as to not spook game. Slimmer cuts and strategic designs eliminate that Stay Puft Marshmallow Man look and fit. One thing that hasn't changed: Fashion still matters, probably even more so today when logos sell more clothing than the actual features do.

PERSPECTIVE

Take a look at the Cabela's catalog—natural materials are in again. Without exception, merino wool is still the best base layer, and new waterproofing treatments are helping down make a comeback as the warm, lightweight insulation of choice. However, when it comes to shell materials, synthetic laminates are lighter, quieter, more waterproof, and all-around better than oilskin. The wise hunter will look beyond the marketing hype and build a clothing system accordingly, but whatever material he chooses, it's still smart to live by one cardinal rule: cotton kills.

TRACK A DEER WITH A STICK
When trying to track a wounded animal, the best tool a hunter can have is a stride stick. Find a sapling four to five feet long, and trim it of branches. Measure the distance between two known tracks and mark a notch into the stick. When tracking becomes difficult over tough terrain, put the notch in the last known track and swipe the point of the stick in an arc to pick up the next track, or slight soil disturbance, before moving forward to find the next spot. This technique can save the day and help you find that buck.

DRINK FROM A STREAM
Many hunters carry bottled water or water in a spare bladder. At six pounds a gallon, this is not your best option for deep excursions into the wilderness. While drinking right out of a stream is courting giardia and other parasites, carrying an empty water bottle and purification tablets weighs next to nothing and used correctly kills 99.9% of all nasties.

KILL A PREDATOR WITH YOUR HAND
This is an old technique that still works fantastic today. Place the palm of your hand against your mouth while pursing your lips. Suck air between lips and hand to make a mouse squeak or draw it out for a rabbit in distress sound. Many a coyote has met its demise to this field-expedient call, which can be heard over several hundred yards on a still day.

FIREMAKING

FLINT & STEEL VS LIGHTER

With a piece of flint and a bit of steel, along with cattail down and pine resin, the woodsman walks confidently into the field ready for anything, knowing a crackling campfire is just a spark away. Barring flint, he builds a bow drill from tree limbs and cordage, spinning his way to fire, or, at the very least, works up enough body heat trying to warm up. Going even further back in history, the ancient hunter knew carrying fire was easier than building it, so he packed away a glowing ember wrapped tightly, ready to grow into a flame with the addition of tinder and a few well-directed breaths.

The modern hunter with a lighter or waterproof matches in his pocket and a firetab in his pack should be all but guaranteed a fire anytime, anywhere. Add in the convenience of liquid accelerants, better known as a Boy Scout's best friend, and a flick of the thumb produces not just a spark, but a sustained flame capable of igniting all but the wettest of wood. Of course, used carelessly, there's also the likelihood of a trip to the burn unit, but, as a generation more concerned about self-help than survival skills likes to say, with great risks come great rewards.

PERSPECTIVE

Always mind the most important rule of survival and carry at least three ways to start fire while hunting. Matches, lighters, and a spark igniter all qualify, and at least one, along with some type of tinder, should always be carried in a shirt or pants pocket and not in a pack that could become lost. Still, Murphy's Law applies, and the skill to start a fire without matches or a lighter could save a life or, at the very least, make an unplanned night spent in the woods more comfortable.

RANGEFINDING

READING DISTANCE VS ELECTRONIC RANGEFINDERS

Hunters from previous generations didn't have the luxury of an electronic rangefinder. Instead, he was constantly eyeballing distance—and not just when he had a bow or rifle in his hands. On the walk to work, he guessed ranges, confirming them by counting his paces. He also made mental notes of known distances—the height of a telephone pole or length of a football field—and imagined them laid end to end to the animal. He knew the average size of the animal he was hunting, estimating range within his scope or sights in relation to the measurement from the top of the back to its brisket.

Today, a hunter with the push of a button can instantly know a deer is 278 yards away. The size of a deck of cards, next-generation rangefinders can provide an exact point of aim for the cartridge the hunter is shooting and, for the archer, even display the highest arc of his arrow for threading a shot through tight brush. It can tell where to hold when shooting uphill or downhill and at distances most hunters have no business shooting. For the steady shot, a rangefinder virtually eliminates any excuse for missing, and the technology is even built into binoculars, scopes, and bowsights.

PERSPECTIVE

In the field, hunters should use an electronic rangefinder whenever possible to ensure the most accurate and ethical shot. The rest of the year, constant practice judging distance visually with electronic confirmation will make snap-shots easier and ensure a killing shot in those instances a trophy appears out of nowhere, leaving the hunter no time to range it electronically.

PREDATOR CALLING

MOUTH CALLS **VS** E-CALLERS

MOUTH CALLS

Not so long ago—just a few years, in fact—every predator hunter worth his fur wore an open-reed mouth call on a lanyard around his neck. He probably had another one or two, along with a closed-reed call, in a nearby pocket. Much to the annoyance of his spouse, he spent all year practicing with each of them so that at the first set of the season he could go from a jackrabbit squeal to a cottontail in distress to the squeak of a mouse without so much as an extra breath. With the same call he could make a bobcat squall or the yip of a whipped pup and, with the addition of an old cow horn, set every coyote in the county on notice with a convincing howl.

E-CALLERS

Believe everything you read and you could become convinced anyone with a squawk box full of batteries and a chunk of fur on a spring-loaded stick can call in a coyote. Truth be told, even equipped with an electronic caller, the fur hunter is facing the ultimate challenge of trying to lure an animal that survives at the top of the food chain. Still, with a thousand high-definition calls at his fingertips, today's predator hunter does have it easier, dialing through everything from a human baby bawling to—our personal favorite for pranks—the howling housecat-in-heat or about any other sound you can imagine. Most e-callers today aren't content with just providing sound, but movement as well, with what amounts to a stuffed-animal spinning to seal the deal on wary predators.

PERSPECTIVE

Though they might not admit it in public, even the most grizzled of fur traders has an e-caller tucked under the seat of his hunting truck. They're just too versatile to ignore and can make the difference between punching hair and going home with the tail tucked between the legs. But that mouth call still hangs around his neck to provide a finishing note when needed or to fill in holes found in hi-def recordings. Besides, with every amateur out there carrying an e-caller, that mouth call might just give well- educated predators something they've never heard before.

AIMING METHOD

IRON

Romantic is the notion of the prairie hunter, his heavy-barreled rifle propped into the cross-sticks as he squints through the peep sights at a far-off buffalo. His accuracy is near-mythical, as was his ability to wipe out entire herds of animals from one stand, but whether or not those stories are true, it's likely an experienced plainsman could outshoot today's average optics-assisted shooter. Much of that ability comes from practice and the intimate knowledge of how a rifle shoots. He knew to center the post in the peep, rather than bury it at the bottom of the circle, or, with traditional open sights, not to cover the target, but instead place it atop the front blade. Though impervious to the elements, open sights can be hard to adjust perfectly.

VS

OPTICS

Equipped with a high-quality scope and matched rifle, a modern hunter is almost sniper-like. With lots of practice and an understanding of his capabilities (and limits), he is able to ethically kill animals at incredible distances. In dark timber, where he's likely to jump a buck at his feet, he knows to dial his scope down for the widest possible field of view, and when hunting the open country of the West, he can up the magnification to nearly pick the very hair he plans to split on his target. Today's scopes offer today's hunters with any number of crystal-clear sight pictures, from standard duplex crosshairs to electronic dots to ballistic-compensating reticles measured in mil-dots or, yes, even inches to compensate for both drop and wind drift.

PERSPECTIVE

When it comes down to it, sights are all about personal preference. A hunter whose nerves are amplified by the magnified crosshairs bouncing wildly may be able to cut playing cards with a peep sight, while aging hunters may struggle to keep everything in focus with open sights. In short, hunters should be proficient with each. Particularly, those who prefer a scoped rifle should at least practice with open sights in the not-so-unlikely event their optics should break in the field. Either way, accurate shooting is less about what sights are used and more about measured breathing, steady holds, and trigger control. Ⓗ

Packing Meat

Learning to quarter, bone, and pack meat in the field is one of the oldest skills every hunter should know.

When it comes time to get the edible parts off a game animal you've just dropped in wilderness country, throw out the standard butchering practices often used for whitetails (skin on, gut, drag 100 yards to truck and take to butcher). Far from a road, there is seldom a need to gut an animal as it is likely going out in game bags. The steps are simple: Get the skin off of one side quickly (caping the front half if you plan to mount the animal) and lift the quarters off of that half of the carcass. Fillet the backstraps and neck and trim the ribs down to the bone. Roll the carcass over onto the laid-out hide and repeat.

Quartering is easier than it sounds. At the front, just lift the leg and slash through the armpit. As you do so, the shoulder will lift farther away from the carcass. Keep slicing, cutting close to the rib cage to keep meat with the front quarter. There is no joint connecting a front shoulder to an animal; just cut through the connective muscle and tissue and voila! You've got a free quarter.

Rear quarters are attached a bit more firmly. Probe out the contour of the spine, pelvis, and hip; sink your knife in and cut the heavy muscle free from them. Topside pre-cuts complete, lift the rear leg and carve away at the connecting tissues in the groin area, being careful not to slice the intestines. Soon you'll find the hip joint; cut the sinews that attach the hip ball and work through and around it. At this point work your way up along the planes and contours of the pelvis until you meet the topside pre-cuts, then lift the quarter off.

Hang all this bloody goodness in the shade, preferably where a bit of breeze can reach them, to start cooling while you then—and only then—go into the guts for the tenderloins.

A slit in the abdomen just below the spine will allow you to access and lift out the tenderloins, and if you want the kidneys, liver, and heart, you can get to them through it as well.

Put each quarter in a separate game bag and stick the backstraps, tenderloins, trim, and neck meat in another. Hanging them across a tree branch to cool and dry a bit prior to bagging them makes for less mess and cleaner, less sticky meat.

At this point, you're ready to load your meat onto a packhorse or—where legal and ethically accessible—onto an ATV. However, if you're backpacking, you've still got some work to do.

Nobody in their right mind carries heavy bones out on their own back unless the hike is short. Now is the time to bone that meat out.

There's no need to carefully cut each quarter up into roasts and whatnot; just pare the meat away from the bone in one big layer. Rear quarters are easy; front shoulders—specifically the shoulder blade—are a bit more technical. It's not hard, it just takes time, and when you heave your pack aboard, you'll bless the many pounds you've left behind in the form of bones.

If you prefer not to bloody your pack, drop the boned-out meat into game bags, then into heavy-duty plastic garbage bags. Plastic isn't good for long-term storage of raw meat—it slows cooling and can promote bacteria growth—but the meat's going to be smushed inside your pack where it can't breathe anyway, right? For the short term, plastic works fine and keeps your pack clean.

As a bonus, if you're camped along a cold, flowing creek, you can drop the plastic-bagged meat right into the water, which will cool it aggressively and preserve it for several days—a real boon in hot weather. Be sure to anchor it to creek-side bushes to prevent it from drifting away.

CARRYING CAPACITY

When the meat is traveling out aboard your shoulders, the size of the animal you've just turned into future culinary bliss has a huge impact on the packing-out process. One sturdy fellow in good condition can pack a boned-out mule deer, cape, and antlers out of wilderness country in a single trip if he really wants to. However, if you've just dropped an elk—or worse, a moose—you've got your work cut out for you, particularly if the weather is warm.

A hunter in good condition can carry about 50 to 70 pounds of dead weight, as long as the terrain isn't too technical, over a series of trips. Carry much more than that and you'll waste yourself in one trip.

A big, mature bull elk can yield upward of 300 pounds of pure, boned-out meat. Even a young spike bull can give up 200 pounds or more. Do the math—unless you've got good help, you're in for a multiple-day job. Working alone on a moose that you dropped five or six miles from the trailhead could take a week of work to get it all out.

If the weather is cold, below freezing at night and not more than 45 degrees during the heat of the day, packing out is much simpler because you can take your time. Hung in the shade, meat will partially freeze during the night and stay cool all day. However, if it's hot you've got to work hard and fast—and call help. Early-season bowhunts are the most problematic; daytime temperatures can reach the mid-80s even in alpine country. Before dropping the hammer on a moose or other such behemoths, you owe it to the animal to consider several things. How far are you from the trailhead, how warm is the weather, and will you have help hauling? You may be just too far, or the weather just too warm, to allow you to get all the meat out before it spoils—if so, pass the shot.

Ethically—and in some areas, legally—hauling the meat first and the antlers and cape out last is the right thing to do. In Alaska, you'd better get every last scrap of edible meat off that carcass: You can get a whopper ticket and have your trophy confiscated if you get lax.

What about ribs? I'm as much a fan of barbecued ribs as the next guy, but if I'm boning out an animal for a long pack out, I leave the ribs after paring the meat close to the bone. Birds and other small wilderness scavengers need to eat, too. But check local laws and pack the ribs out if required.

PACKS

The first step toward success is having a good pack that freights meat well. Daypacks are all but useless, and even top-quality mountaineering-type internal-frame packs aren't optimal. For pure packing purposes, a premium external pack frame that you can simply lash quarters and game bags to is ideal. I've used a Frontier Gear of Alaska pack from Barney's Sports

As you quarter an animal prior to packing, hang the quarters in a shady place to drip dry and cool.

Chalet with great success.

However, it's ludicrous to expect wilderness hunters to haul an external-frame freighter pack around while hunting, so the best bet is a heavy-duty, large-capacity internal frame pack with a very good hip belt. Kuiu's Icon Pro 7200 is a great option, as is Eberlestock's V90 Battleship. Such a pack will get you, your meat, and your camp out to civilization, and when not full with gear and meat, it can be collapsed in size to make day hunts easier while wearing it.

BEAR PROTECTION

Most moose hunting and much elk hunting is done in grizzly country, and no bear is above a free steak dinner. After quartering or boning-out your animal, hang meat sacks away from the carcass, preferably 100 yards or more. Ideally, hang them high on a cross pole in a location you can observe as you approach. Keep an eye on the carcass, too, and use caution as you load your pack with meat and head back toward the trailhead. And it doesn't hurt to hang a can of bear spray on the front of your hip belt—it has been proven on numerous encounters with bears and is often a great first line of defense. Ⓗ

BEAR ATTACKS:

ARE YOU ON THE MENU?

You know that eerie feeling you get as you walk through the woods? The one that seems like someone—or something—is watching you? You may be right. A recent study in Wyoming found that grizzly bears might just be shadowing hunters.

Biologists with the Interagency Grizzly Bear Study Team (IGBST) fitted eight Wyoming grizzlies with GPS collars last summer and followed their movements throughout hunting season. The researchers also gave GPS devices to 100 volunteer hunters. They then compared movements of the bears in relation to the hunters' activity.

One grizzly appeared to follow a group of elk hunters from as little as 100 yards away, staying downwind of them as they searched for elk. The bear stopped moving for several hours, but picked up the hunters' trail and followed them again. The group never knew the bear was there. ➤

Illustration by Sean Delonas

▶▶ At least that's what it seemed like. Frank van Manen, team leader of the IGBST, says there is really no way to know if the bear was actually following the hunters.

"That could be one interpretation," he says. "It could have just been there at the same time and walking in the same general location. We'll never know for sure."

What van Manen and fellow researchers do know is that grizzly bears and hunters are meeting in the woods more frequently than ever. In most cases, the bear or the hunter retreats, or more likely, the hunter never even knew the bear was around. However, a growing number of bear encounters end with a dead or injured bear or worse, a dead or injured hunter.

That's likely nothing more than a matter of numbers figures van Manen. Grizzly populations in the northern Rocky Mountains are higher than in recent history, so it's not surprising that more encounters are taking place. As many as 1,000 grizzlies live in the greater Yellowstone area, nearly as many live in other parts of Wyoming, Idaho, and Montana. Virtually all of them inhabit elk country.

"Part of the study is aimed at learning how we can reduce conflicts between bears and hunters," van Manen says. "We know grizzlies are attracted to carcasses and gut piles. One bear traveled 10 miles in a straight line to an elk carcass. That's how good their sense of smell is. Are hunters at a greater risk when they've killed an elk? Does the sound of a gunshot trigger a response in bears? Does hunting activity draw bears from other areas, increasing the chance of a run-in?"

The good news is that hunters seem to be at a lower risk than non-hunters. Of the approximately 50 people killed by grizzlies in North America since 1970, just 10 were known to be hunting. Nearly half of all fatal attacks occurred in national or provincial parks or refuges; most are closed to hunting. Those statistics can be misleading, says U.S. Fish and Wildlife Service Grizzly Bear Recovery Coordinator Chris Servheen.

"I don't think you can draw a conclusion that hunters are safer based on those numbers," he says. "Hunters are doing the very things we tell people not to do in grizzly country. They move very quietly, they are active at dusk and dawn, and they often travel alone. Quite a few have been attacked, and several have been killed."

In many instances, those hunters were carrying or standing over a freshly killed animal. A 53-year-old Tennessee man was killed in Northwest Territories in September 2014 as he was cutting up a moose. Another hunter was killed in Montana in 2001 as he field-dressed an elk, the only hunter attacked and killed in the Lower 48 since 1970. More recently, a man was severely injured when he and some friends were attacked by as many as five bears as they packed out a deer on Sally Island, Alaska.

Just as encounters with grizzlies are on the rise, run-ins with black bears are also trending upward. Statistically, however, they are less likely to attack a human. Just 38 people have been killed by wild black bears throughout North America since 1970, including 11 in the contiguous United States. Estimates vary, but researchers think there are nearly one million black bears in North America, with as many as 300,000 living in the contiguous United States alone.

None of those killed were hunting, but there have been numerous reports of attacks on hunters in recent years. A Minnesota bowhunter was mauled in September 2014 by a bear he was tracking after he shot it. He not only survived, he actually killed the bear with a knife, despite being severely injured. A Washington hunter was bitten on the leg after being chased up a tree, also in September, and an Alberta hunter was attacked by a wounded black bear last August.

"There is an increasing overlap in bear range and human range. Black bear numbers are up throughout much of their range, and so is the human population," says Minnesota Department of Natural Resources Bear Project Leader Dave Garshelis. "The increase in conflicts is really just a matter of numbers."

University of Calgary professor emeritus Dr. Stephen Herrero coauthored a research paper titled "Fatal Attacks by American Black Bear on People: 1900–2009." He found a clear pattern: Most people who were attacked were alone. And contrary to popular belief, females with cubs are far less likely to attack than males.

"The bears that occasionally kill people …do it very stealthily. They get close to a person and then they charge, usually without making any noise," says Herrero in a video interview posted on-line.

Grizzlies, on the other hand, tend to attack as a defensive mechanism, says Servheen. They are guarding food or their cubs or they perceive a human as some sort of territorial threat. That's why backcountry hunters need to be watching for more than elk or deer or moose. They need to watch for bears and bear sign.

BEAR SPRAY VS. GUNS

U.S. Fish and Wildlife service law enforcement personnel examined encounters with bears dating back to 1992 in which pepper spray was used and compared them to attacks where guns were used in self-defense. Contrary to popular belief, those who used pepper spray were less likely to be injured.

According to the report, "…persons encountering grizzlies and defending themselves with firearms suffer injury about 50 percent of the time. During the same period, persons defending themselves with pepper spray escaped injury most of the time, and those that were injured experienced shorter duration attacks and less severe injuries. Canadian bear biologist Dr. Stephen Herrero reached similar conclusions based on his own research—a person's chance of incurring serious injury from a charging grizzly doubles when bullets are fired versus when bear spray is used."

U.S. Fish and Wildlife Service bear biologist Chris Servheen used to carry a handgun when he works or hunts in bear country, but not anymore.

"It's easier to hit a bear with spray than a pistol," he says. "Just make sure you keep the spray somewhere that it is readily available. It won't do you any good if you can't reach it in a hurry."

"I always recommend hunting with a partner. The more eyes you have, the better, and you'll appear like a bigger threat to a bear," he adds. "If you kill something, get it out quickly or be cautious if you have to leave it and come back and retrieve it."

And don't forget to glance behind you every once in a while. Just because you are paranoid doesn't mean something isn't following you. — *David Hart*

Tough & Tiny Coues Whitetail

Here's how to get your feet wet hunting the world's most interesting, challenging whitetail deer.

Coues deer are tiny, desert-dwelling siblings of the common whitetail. Properly, they are simply a subspecies, *Odocoileus virginianus couesi,* but their habits and the landscape in which they live set them apart.

You can't hunt them like typical whitetails—coues country is too big and too wide-open. You've got to be able to glass well, stalk long, and shoot precisely. If you want a coues whitetail, you'll have to shake off the lazy conventions ingrained by too many years of sitting in tree stands and actually hunt.

Imagine a cagey old whitetail doe crossbred with the toughest desert bighorn out there, and you'll have a glimmering of what a big coues buck is like.

The best hunting is found in Mexico, where vast private ranches offer little-disturbed populations of deer with exceptional genetics. But hunting Mexico is expensive and dangerous. Stateside, the desert country of southern Arizona holds an estimated 85,000 coues deer, according to Big Game Management Supervisor Amber Munig—perfect for a public-land DIY hunt.

To access good hunting, aggressive backcountry wilderness techniques are demanded. Trophy hunters leave roads and vehicles behind and penetrate as deep as their physical conditioning and desert-specialized backpacking equipment will take them.

TAGS AND ACCESS

Arizona tags must be obtained through a draw. But if you'd rather get tough and hunt a third- or fourth-choice area, you can draw and hunt every year. If you prefer to apply for only the best areas, you'll draw only occasionally, but when you do draw, you'll hunt where populations are large and bucks are plentiful.

Access to some units can be problematic; a call to a biologist in southern Arizona will help you sort through the best units to apply for as well as good second, third, and so forth options, and assist you in navigating access.

WITHOUT QUALITY GLASS—AND THE RIGHT TYPE OF QUALITY GLASS—YOU'LL FAIL.

Parts of New Mexico have good coues deer hunting as well. According to state Big Game Program Manager Stewart Liley, "Coues deer in New Mexico get really overlooked. They provide a very unique opportunity, and a few hunters really key into it." New Mexico tags are also draw-only, but there are often leftover tags, and if you can obtain permission on private property, over-the-counter, either-species (mule deer and coues deer) tags are available. For the best coues hunting, try the Burro Mountains, Peloncillo Mountains, and the southern part of the Gila.

GLASSING

Using your eyes is key to finding coues deer. The desert country they inhabit is vast, deer numbers are few, and picking apart the terrain and sifting through the scattered does until you find a mature, huntable buck comprises the majority of the hunt. Prepare physically and mentally for predawn hikes up ridges and canyon walls to access vantage points and for hours of carefully glassing as the sun comes up and paints the desert vermillion, then fades into brassy skies.

Without quality glass—and the right type of quality glass—you'll fail. Hours of peering through subpar binoculars will cause eyestrain and headaches, entirely aside from proving unsatisfactory for picking apart the details of the landscape and finding deer.

Decades ago fanatical coues deer hunters began using 15X binoculars mounted on homemade tripod adapters. Such rigs proved so superior for finding the tiny, smoke-colored deer that today almost all serious coues hunters use them.

Premium models, such as the Zeiss Conquest HD 15x56, are ideal; I used these and they are superb. Plus, they come with a very cool, quick-detach tripod adapter—ideal for long days sitting behind them.

Don't skyline yourself (coues deer see abnormally well) and get comfortable when glassing. In early morning, watch for sudden movement as young deer dash around to shake off the night's chill and for glowing bodies as deer cross splashes of sunlight among the shadows. In the afternoon, glass shaded areas and spots of shadow under solitary trees.

As evening comes, watch for movement as deer get up and wander in lengthening shadows on north- and east-facing slopes. During the early seasons, mature bucks tend to run alone or in small bachelor groups and like to bed in isolated areas where small spots of shade form in the afternoon. Pay particular attention to glassing beneath ledges and cliff faces.

Rut activity warms up in December, and bucks become more visible as they prowl and chase does. According to Mike Jensen, who grew up hunting and guiding for coues deer in Arizona and who happens to also be the president of Zeiss USA, unlike typical whitetail bucks that prowl continuously and lock down with individual does, rutting coues bucks tend to gather harems and stick with them, working them like a bull elk works his harem and fighting off satellite bucks. If you're lucky enough to land a tag for the late season, glass hard around every group of does—a buck will be lurking nearby.

CLOTHING AND BOOTS

Wear light, breathable clothing that resists tearing and thorns, cactus needles, and burrs. I had to throw away my favorite pair of quiet, flex-fabric hunting pants after our hunt last fall because of the hundreds of tiny, hair-like cactus needles that became permanently imbedded in the pant legs over the course of the hunt.

Wear layers. I prefer a thin, wicking underlayer (make sure it's a suitable camo pattern because it's likely all you'll wear on your upper body during the heat of the day), a good thorn- and tear-resistant long-sleeve shirt with ample pockets, topped with a packable down jacket to ward off the chill of the morning.

For boots, choose something light, and breathability is more important than waterproofing. Ankle support is vital to many folks; personally, I go for boots that offer me the surest grip on loose rock and while climbing sandstone ledges. Danner's Tachyon boots weigh a ridiculously light 26 ounces, breathe well, and grip uncertain terrain better than anything else I've used. They offer little ankle support, they aren't waterproof, and I've had mesquite thorns penetrate fully through the soles. Being so light they aren't the most robust of boots—I'll destroy a pair in a season's worth of hunting—but they are quiet, my feet love them, and I don't often fall or slip in them.

PACKS, TENTS, AND SLEEPING BAGS

Some coues hunters—such as Jensen and his son, Garrett—are tougher than me and will sleep in a light sleeping bag wrapped in a tarp to keep the dew off. Me, I don't like nighttime visitors, and since coues country is typically home to scorpions, rattlesnakes, tarantulas, and other warmth-loving creatures of the night, I prefer a light single-wall tent. If you hunt with a partner, choose a two- or three-man model and split the load. For a couple of pounds each, you can stay out of the wind, sand, and creepy crawlies.

Although daytime temperatures can reach the 90s during a hot hunt, desert nights can be piercingly cold. I prefer down-filled sleeping bags, such as the KUIU Super Down, with a water-resistant shell that pack tiny and are rated to 15 degrees or less. They're expensive, yes, but so is your hunt, and good rest at night will enable you to hunt harder and more efficiently. I pair my bag with a 14-ounce ExPed Synmat pad.

Finally, you'll need a mountaineering-quality pack suitable for hunting. I use a Sitka 45, which is light and tough, has just enough internal capacity, and sports a decent rifle suspension system for those times when you need to strap your rifle to your pack.

RIFLE AND SCOPE

Coues deer are small to begin with and are usually shot at much greater distances than typical whitetails or even mule deer. Choose a rifle that shoots very, very accurately, in a caliber that shoots very flat. On today's market, there is perhaps no more perfect coues deer cartridge than the new 26 Nosler, loaded with an aerodynamic hunting bullet.

Light rifle weight is also important. Although coues deer don't live at extreme elevations like bighorn sheep and mountain goats, the terrain they inhabit is unforgiving, and a featherweight rifle that offers superb accuracy is a quantifiable advantage. My go-to coues gun is a Rifle's Inc. Strata. With a skeletonized action, custom barrel, and proprietary stock, it weighs 6.5 pounds with scope and shoots half-MOA with the right ammo.

Choosing the right scope is also critical. It should be light yet offer either a capable ballistic reticle or the ability to dial the elevation turret for distant shots. Zeiss's Conquest HD5 in 3-15x42, with the company's Rapid-Z 800 reticle, is awfully tough to beat. Correctly used, it equips you to drop a coues whitetail from spitting distance to the outside edge of your shooting ability, whether that's 300 or 600 yards.

BORDER DANGER

Coues country is border country, and some areas experience high traffic by illegals. Encounters are rare, and most such desert nomads are nonaggressive and thirsty. Hide your camps to minimize theft risk. ⬣

OPPORTUNITY
ALBER

UNDERRATED NORTHWESTERN MOUNTAINS PROVIDE A TOUGH WINTER TEST.

TA

ALBERTA'S NOVEMBER cold bit at my cheeks and instantly froze the hairs inside my nose when I stepped from the hail-dappled old Suburban, but there was a mature bull moose away across 600 yards of muskeg and alders and we couldn't stalk him while sitting in the truck. I screwed my hat on a bit tighter, shrugged my T/C Dimension rifle across my shoulder, and followed my guide into knee-deep snow.

We were hunting the late season, long after the bulls quit rutting and became uncallable. Heated trucks enabled survival as we covered vast stretches of frozen boreal forest, chaining up to drive logging roads to high spots, where we glassed logging clear-cuts and valley swamps in search of big bulls.

Uncharacteristically for late fall, the bull we'd just found was with cows, which made me suspect his maturity. But Alberta guide Grayson Bunnage left no doubt that this was a bull we had to try for.

The snow was deep but powdery and quiet, courtesy of a cold too frigid to allow the surface to melt in the daylight sun and freeze-form a crust at night. Soundlessly, we wallowed through it, praying that the marginal cross-breeze wouldn't shift and carry our scent to the moose. Circling to get the wind in our faces was out of the question—it would require more time and strength than we had.

JOSEPH VON BENEDIKT

SURE ENOUGH

Open areas like this
hold moose—the trick to
finding them is to cover and
glass a lot of country.

, as we neared the spot we hoped to set up and shoot from, the wind suddenly left my burning right ear, hesitated as if unsure of the ethics of what it was about to do, and then blew full on the back of my neck. I rose slightly from my crouch and peeked over the covering alders just in time to see the moose fade into the black conifers beyond.

Standing an average of six feet, six inches at the shoulder, *Alces alces andersoni*—more commonly known by its blue-collar name of Canada moose— bulls have very long legs and broad hooves well suited to navigating waterlogged tundra swamps and deep snow. In a walking competition, we didn't have a chance. We reversed and began the 20-minute, 400-yard trek back to the Suburban.

In Alberta, moose can be hunted in the foothills of the Rockies for about the same price as a decent elk hunt, and a whitetail or mule deer tag can be added for peanuts. Throw down for a wolf license and you've got a very intriguing multiple-species package.

This particular hunt was with Todd Bunnage of Rugged Outfitting (ruggedoutfitting.com), located northwest of Calgary. Bunnage's late-season moose hunts come in two guises: a meat hunt for the small bulls plentiful in the valley farmlands and a trophy bull hunt in the mountainous "public" Crown Land, where he is issued a certain amount of outfitter-type tags each year. While he doesn't encourage hunters to expect to shoot a 50-inch bull (which is the equivalent of a 60-plus-inch Alaska-Yukon bull), his hunters do take one or more per year, and as an indication of the quality of his area, locals put in for 10 years or more before earning enough points to draw a resident tag there.

The rifle I shook free of snow and scraped thumbnails-full of ice from back at the truck was T/C's innovative, bolt-action, interchangeable-barrel Dimension model. Anticipating the opportunity to hunt big northern whitetails if I was able to take a moose early enough in my hunt, I'd brought along a .270 Winchester-caliber barrel in addition to the .300 Win. Mag. barrel currently mounted to my action.

Initially ambivalent in my appreciation of the design, I'd found while sighting-in and load testing that both barrels consistently turned in sub-MOA accuracy—a factor I find rather endearing in a production-model hunting rifle. Bolt travel is smooth, function is reliable, and while I still am not in love with the modernistic appearance of the stock, I came to value the Dimension as a precision tool.

Bunnage fired up the Suburban, cranked the heater, and we prowled down the snowpacked logging road. Sweated up from heaving through the drifts, I rolled down my window and sucked in the frigid air.

Ahead a mile and well around and above the copse of pines that the moose had vanished into, Bunnage slowed, searching the treeline below. Adrenaline jangled through me as he slammed on the brakes and pointed at dark forms shadowing the logging cut. Quietly, he cut the motor, and we slipped out the doors to try again.

I don't particularly like hunting from vehicles, and I refuse to shoot an animal out of a truck window even where legal. However, this hunt entailed a lot of hiking to vantage points and glassing, followed by on-foot pursuit when moose were found. Those tactics, combined with the deep, heavy snow and cold, make for a real hunt that rarely results in drive-by type opportunities. Who was I to complain if this time the moose were already almost in range? Quickly, I moved through the snow to gain a few yards, throwing the rifle to my shoulder as the

bull wafted through strings of saplings at the forest's edge. Binocular to his eyes beside me, Bunnage breathed,

"IT'S THE SAME BULL". "YOU SURE OF HIM?" "YES. HE'S SOLID."

~

Standing in the snow, crosshairs glued to the bull's shoulder where he stood glaring some 140 yards distant, I pressed the trigger. The .300 roared, and the distinct whap of a bullet impacting vitals returned across the broken muskeg.

Moose have slow nervous systems, and the bull simply turned slightly, showing little sign of being hit. Never one to miss an opportunity, I racked the bolt and sent another 180-grain Federal Trophy Copper bullet through his ribs, then a third into his shoulder. Clouds of snow frothed as the bull ran sideways and toppled into the deep powder, only one antler showing above the logging off-cuts scattered at the forest's edge.

As we approached him, the bull grew, gaining paddle depth and width over what I thought I'd seen through my binoculars. We scooped the caked snow from his antlers and heaved him into position for photography, hurrying in the cold.

Late-season bull moose are different creatures than the firebreathing monsters of the rut. They are focused on resting, feeding, and replenishing against the coming winter.

~

T/C'S DIMENSION RIFLE

LEGENDARY FOR ITS VERY SUCCESSFUL INTERCHANGEABLE-BARREL SINGLE-SHOT RIFLES, SUCH AS THE CONTENDER, CONTENDER II AND ENCORE...

Extracting a heavy-bodied bull in sub-zero temperatures is made easier by knowledge coupled with the right equipment.

THOMPSON/CENTER is a company that has always pushed the boundaries of versatility. With its new bolt-action, repeating Dimension model, it offers hunters on a budget the opportunity to own a single rifle with multiple barrels.

CNC-machined to very tight tolerances to enable bolt interchangeability (between appropriate calibers with like-size case heads) and consistent repeatability, Dimension rifles utilize a set of letter-coded parts groups to enable shooters to shoot cartridges in four different case families: those based on magnum case heads, those derived from the .30-06 case family, those engineered on the .308 case family, and those based on .223-size cases.

For example, to switch from a .300 Win. Mag. to a .270 Win., as I did during my Alberta moose/whitetail hunt, you'll need two barrels, two bolts, and two magazines. Add a .223-caliber barrel, and you need another bolt and magazine. However, once you're set with the various-size bolts and magazines, you can add barrels. A 7mm Rem. Mag. barrel fits with the magnum bolt and magazine, a .30-06 barrel works with the standard-face bolt and magazine, and so forth. Headspacing is accomplished via very, very precise machining, allowing one bolt to safely serve for multiple (same cartridge family) barrels.

Shooters can choose to hard-mount a scope to their action and simply rezero when mounting a new barrel, or to use a cantilever-type, barrel-mounted scope base on each barrel, with a scope premounted and zeroed. The cantilever system eliminates the need to rezero every time you switch barrels; however, it also makes for a high-mounted optic, reducing the quality of the shooter's cheek weld.

A BASE RIFLE RETAILS FOR $689.
ADDITIONAL BARRELS COST ABOUT $200 AND BOLTS ABOUT $150.

Later, when help arrived, outfitter Todd Bunnage ran an unbelievable length of heavy manila rope from a blue 55-gallon drum—it was literally full of coiled rope—the several hundred yards to my bull, elbowed it around a handy roadside tree stump left from bygone logging days, hooked it to his truck hitch, and drove off down the snow-packed two-track as the guides piloted the bull across the icy muskeg to the road. I'd been anticipating a short but grueling pack; turns out extracting a moose in deep snow can be easy if you're prepared.

I had a whitetail tag in my pocket, and the night after shooting my bull, I'd dug out my extra barrel and the T/C tools needed to swap barrels on the Dimension. The design of the rifle is such that the transition takes less than five minutes to complete. I torqued the barrel nut, bolted the action back into the stock, and confirmed the zero the next morning. Interestingly, Dimension components are machined precisely enough that when remounting a barrel it tends to return to zero well. In this case, 130-grain Sierra

After shooting a bull moose with a .300 Win. Mag. barrel mounted, the author switched his T/C Dimension to a .270 Win. to hunt deer.

GameKings out of Federal Premium factory loads impacted a shade high. A few clicks on my Nikon ProStaff scope and the rifle was ready for business.

Well before dawn, we wound our way through farmland and low-country timber patches. Grayson—a man of few but powerful words—gestured at this pasture corner or that shadowy fencerow with comments such as: "Here's where we saw that 190-class buck last fall." Or: "We had a bowhunter shoot a 168-inch buck right down there last month." With two full days left, I decided to hold out for a big mature deer, putting emphasis on age.

Few thrills can match that of climbing a completely unknown treestand on the edge of the North's promised land and watching early dawn distill across the horizon and drive the wavering Aurora Borealis from the night sky. The snow was less deep than in the mountains—perhaps only 10 inches—but the cold was still intense. Shortly after dawn, three running canine forms burst from a 490-yard-distant treeline, sending an electric burst of adrenaline through me until I realized that they were coyotes, not wolves.

For two hours I saw only a solitary doe feeding in a fringe of trees a half-mile distant. Then three does fed from a black wall of pines 140 yards to my left, eventually bedding just inside the edge of the timber. An optimistic basket-racked eight-point buck swaggered up the treeline and began to harass the does. Suddenly, he boogered like he'd seen a ghost and, considerably deflated, made tracks for parts unknown.

Interested, I glassed the dark pines more closely, finally making out the curve of a main beam and at least two tines of indeterminate length on a bedded deer. The rut was on, and a bigger buck was tending those does from the safety of cover.

Pheromones make fools of the best of us, and the little buck returned, guiltily making his way through scant cover toward the does. I focused my binocular on the bedded buck. Hair raised and posturing like a sure-enough old man of the woods, he emerged stiff-legged from the timber, paralleling the hopeful eight-point, shouldering him away from the does as completely as if he'd been in full contact.

Heavy bodied and long-beamed, dominant and muscled like a professional athlete, he carried what at first looked like a big, nine-point rack. As he stopped in the glow of the morning sun and swung his head, I saw that he was actually a clean 10-point, or would have been had he not broken off the G4 on his left side.

A big, dominant buck, he was no 160-class deer, but the morning was just too perfect. The T/C Dimension coughed and the buck dropped in his tracks, heart and lungs shattered by the Sierra Game-King bullet. I stiffly climbed down the treestand and across the snow to where the buck lay, the ultimate whiteness of the snow beneath him slowly turning crimson.

Several hours existed before my scheduled pickup time. Using the timer on my Nikon camera, I indulged in self-portraits with the buck until the sub-freezing temperatures robbed my camera battery of life. The razor edge of my old Damascus hunting knife made short work of field dressing, and I resolved to drag the buck through the snow and woods to my pickup point.

Even in snow, it was tough to get the heavy old buck moving. Using my belt and rifle sling, I rigged a hip drag and trudged, head down, rifle cradled across my chest, to the snowy two-track through the woods.

Spent, I spread the buck's cavity to drain into the snow and cool, broke a slab of bark to sit on from a decaying tree trunk, and settled in to wait, sunshine vying with the frosty breeze across my face. Ⓗ